7/03

DATE DUE

THE
NEW YORKER
BOOK OF BASEBALL CARTOONS

THE
NEW YORKER
BOOK OF BASEBALL CARTOONS

EDITED BY ROBERT MANKOFF

WITH MICHAEL CRAWFORD

BLOOMBERG PRESS

PRINCETON

PUBLISHED BY BLOOMBERG PRESS

To purchase framed prints of cartoons or to license cartoons for use in periodicals, Web sites, or other media, please contact CARTOONBANK.COM, a New Yorker Magazine company, at 145 Palisade Street, Suite 373, Dobbs Ferry, NY 10522, Tel: 800-897-TOON, or (914) 478-5527, Fax: (914) 478-5604, e-mail: toon@cartoonbank.com, Web: www.cartoonbank.com.

Books are available for bulk purchases at special discounts. Special editions or book excerpts can also be created to specifications. For information, please write: Special Markets Department, Bloomberg Press.

First edition published 2003
1 3 5 7 9 10 8 6 4 2

Library of Congress Cataloging-in-Publication Data

The New Yorker book of baseball cartoons / edited by Robert Mankoff with Michael Crawford.
    p. cm.
    Includes index.
    ISBN 1-57660-127-7 (alk. paper)
    1. Baseball--Caricatures and cartoons. 2. American wit and humor, Pictorial. 3. New Yorker (New York, N.Y. : 1925) I. Title: Book of baseball cartoons, II. Mankoff, Robert III. Crawford, Michael. IV. New Yorker (New York, N.Y. : 1925)
Yorker (New York, N.Y. : 1925)

NC1428.N47 2003
741.5'973--dc21   2002034546

Book design by LAURIE LOHNE / Design It Communications

THE
NEW YORKER
BOOK OF BASEBALL CARTOONS

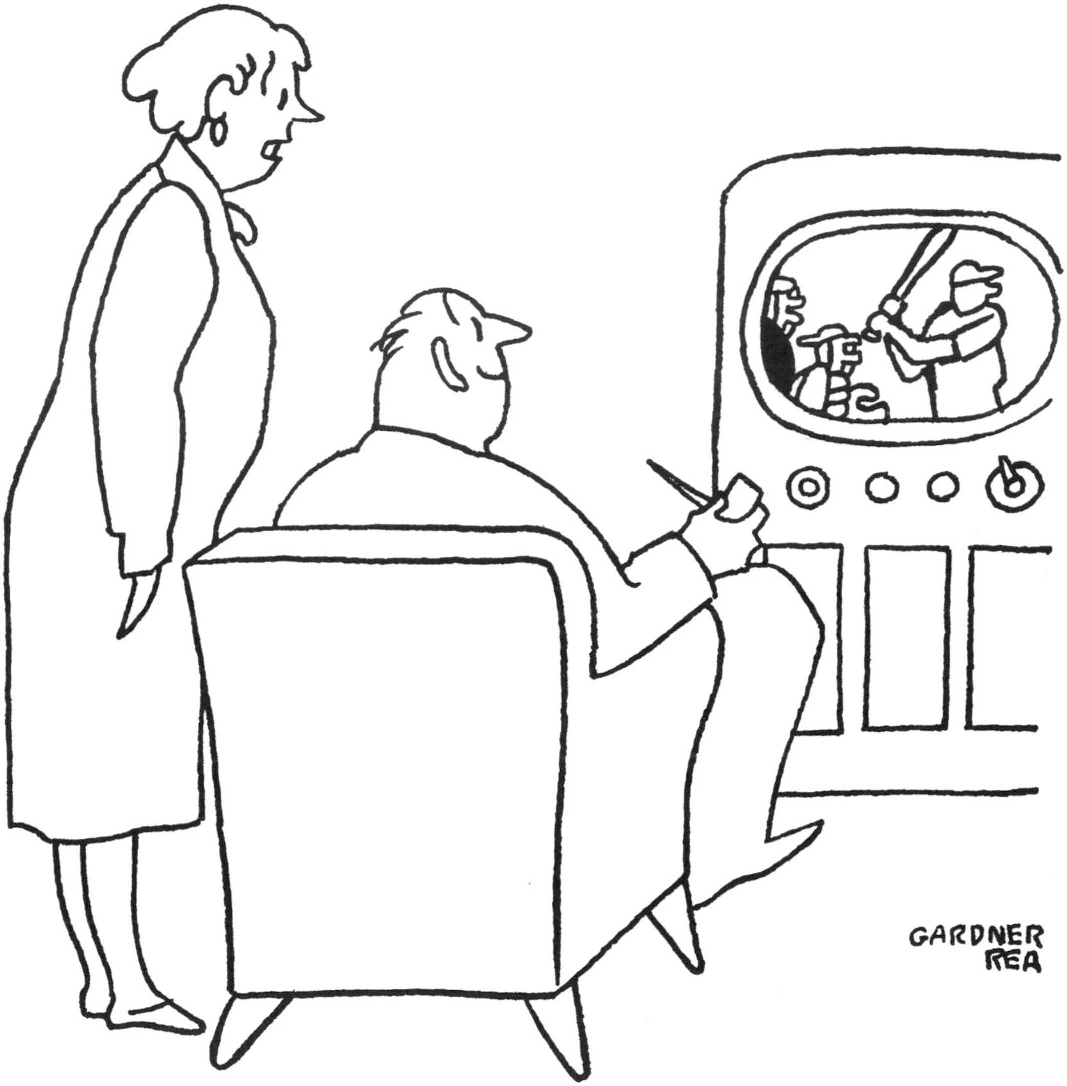
GARDNER
REA

"Oh, no! Not already!"

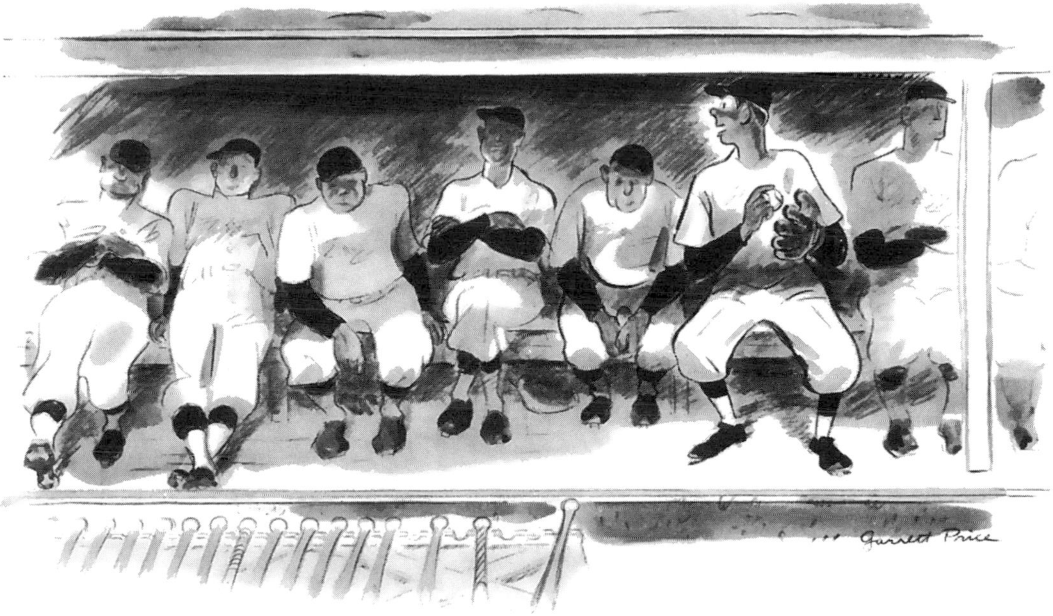
Garrett Price

"Anybody want to play catch?"

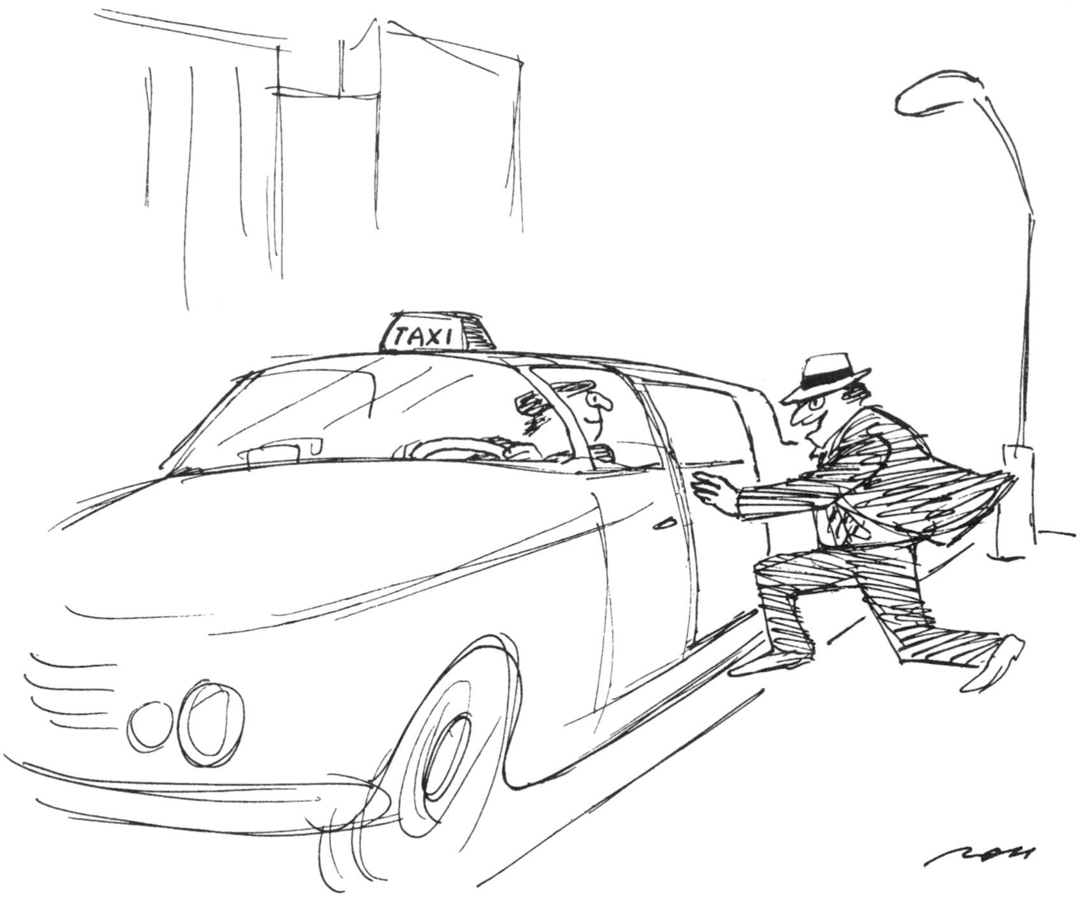
TAXI

"Take me out to the ball game! I don't care if I never get back!"

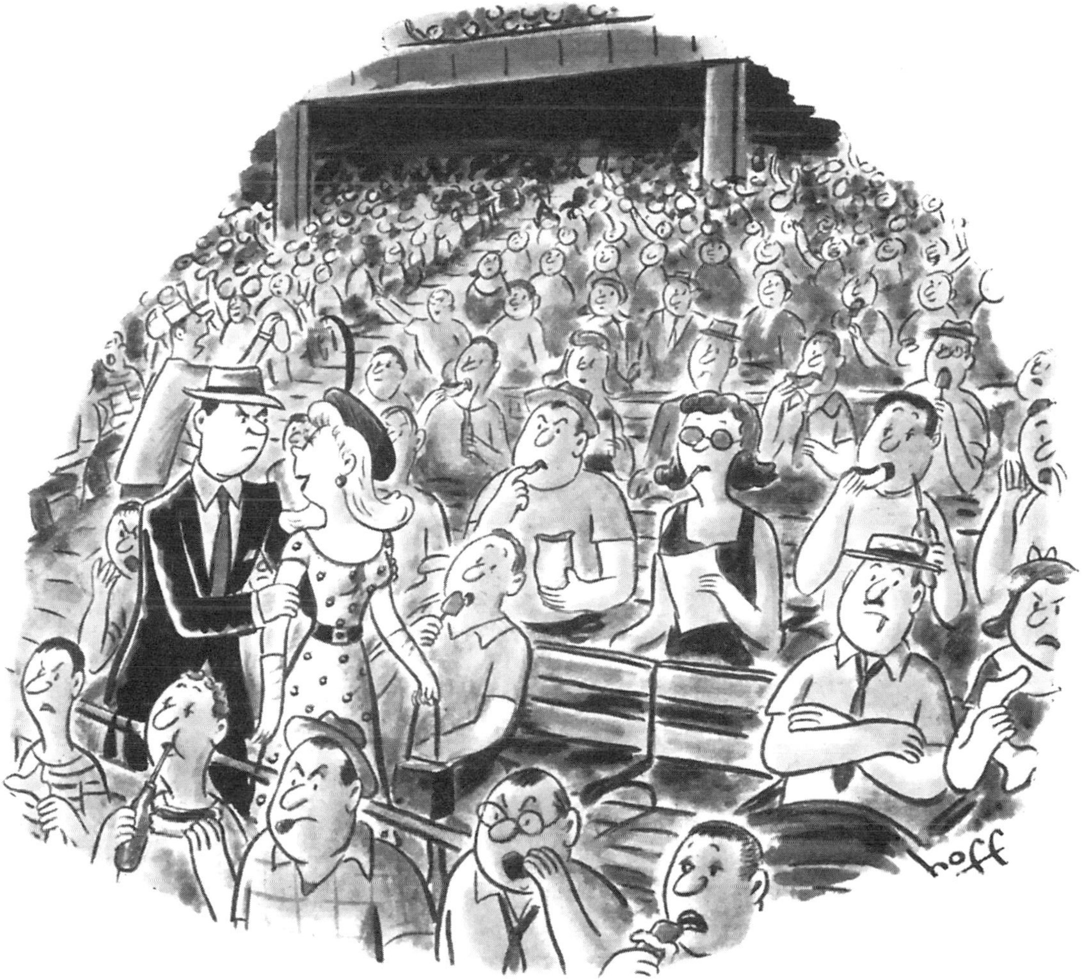
hoff

"See, Grouchy? We haven't missed a thing—the score is still nothing to nothing."

"Sh-h-h! Everyone's staring."

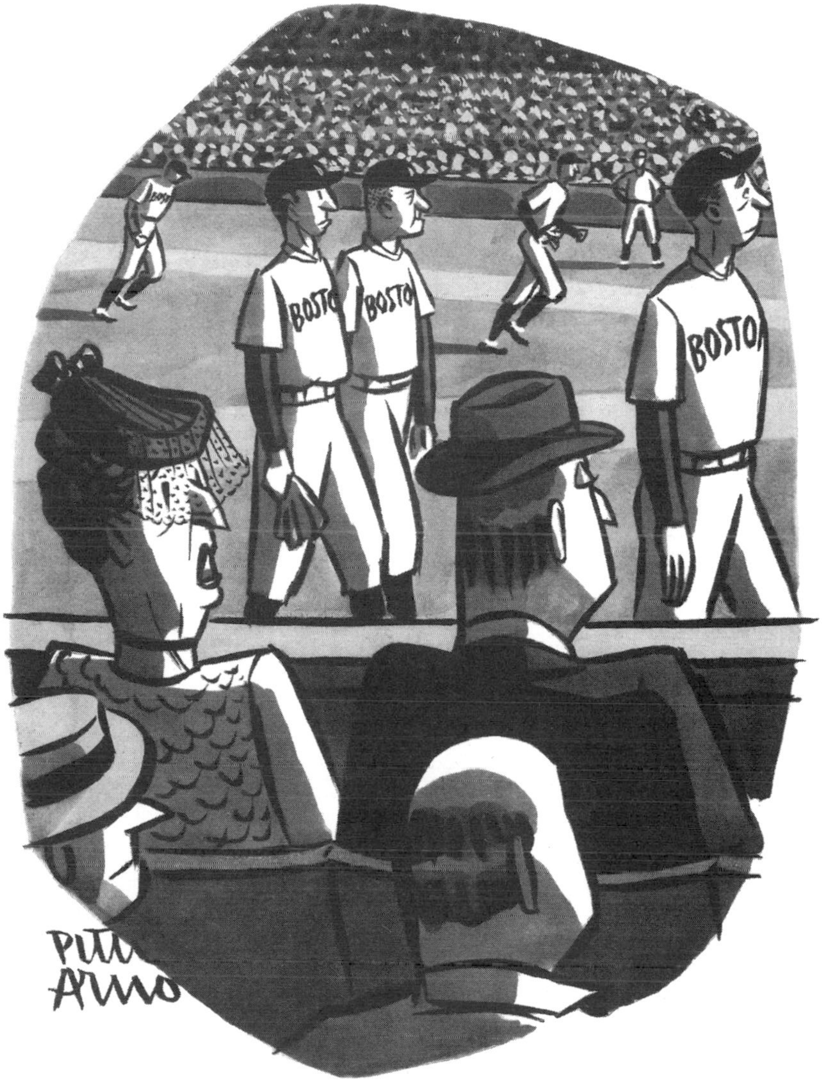
BOSTO
BOSTO
BOSTO

"They don't look Bostonian."

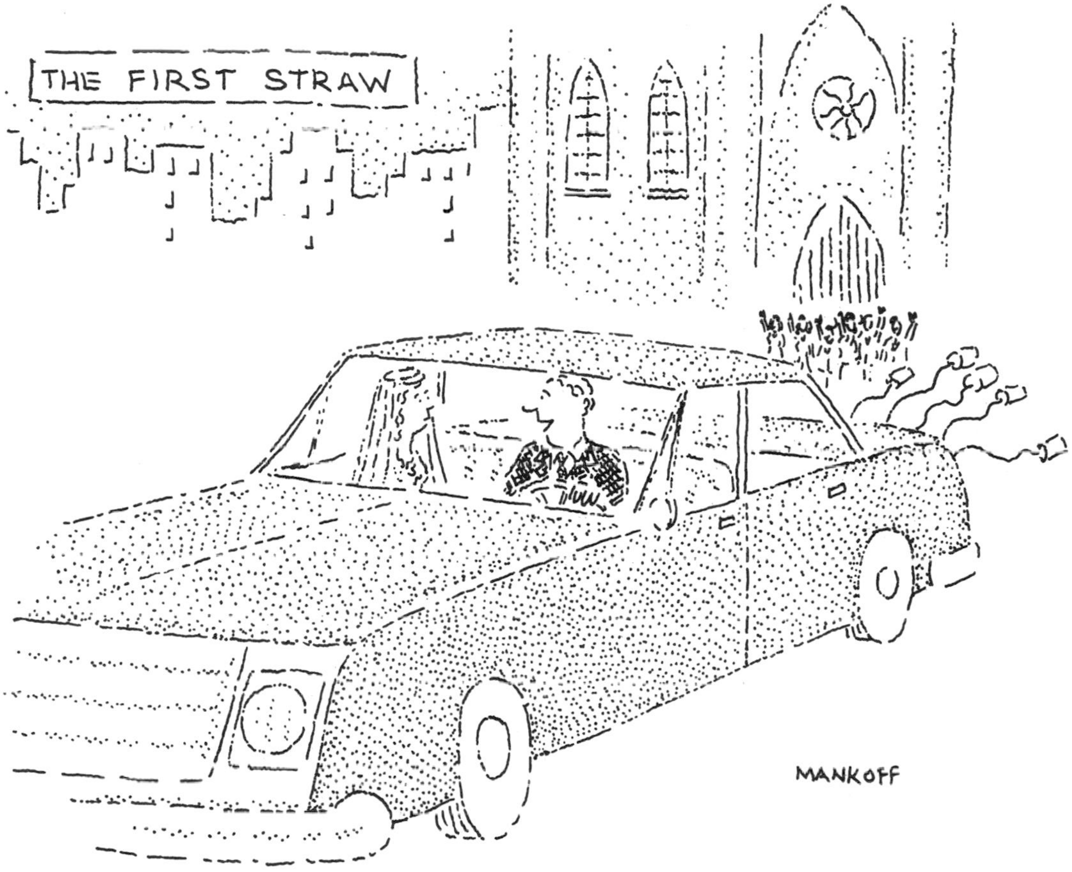
THE FIRST STRAW
MANKOFF

"Mind if I put on the game?"

"Strike him out."

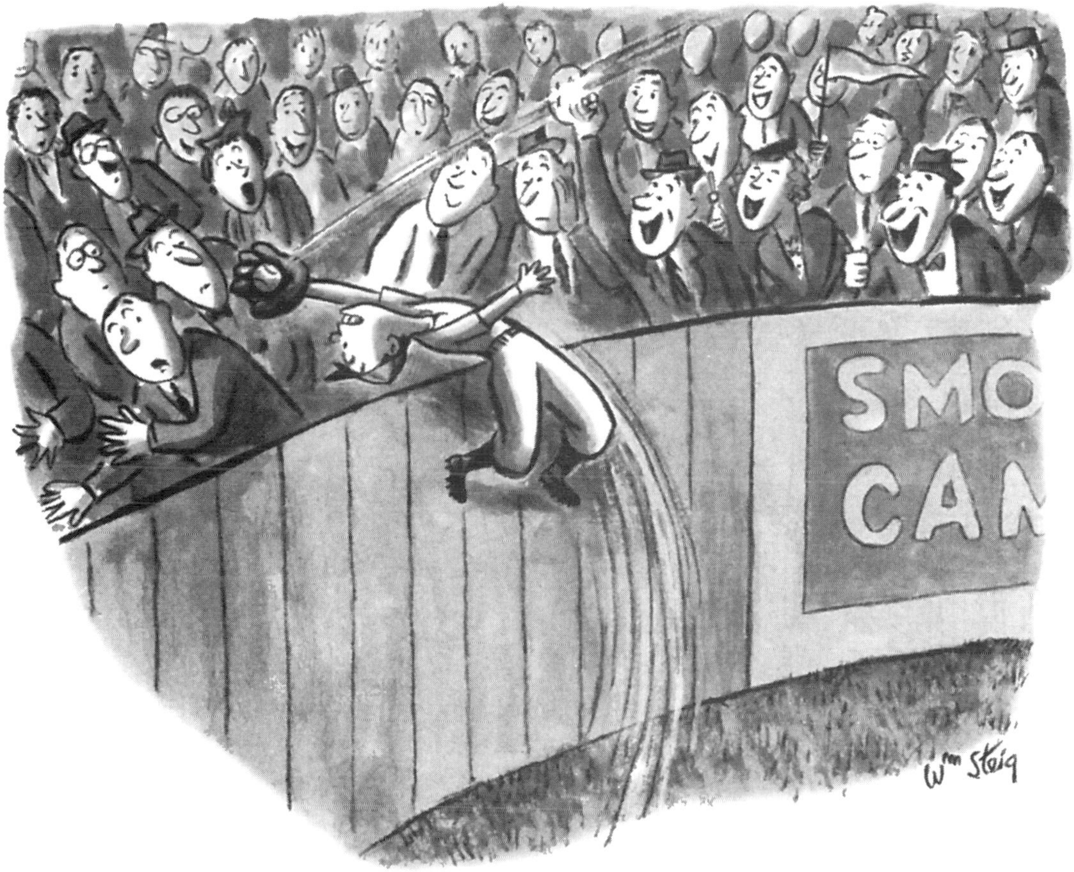
SMO
CAN
Wm Steig

DREAMS OF GLORY

The Catch That Saved The Series

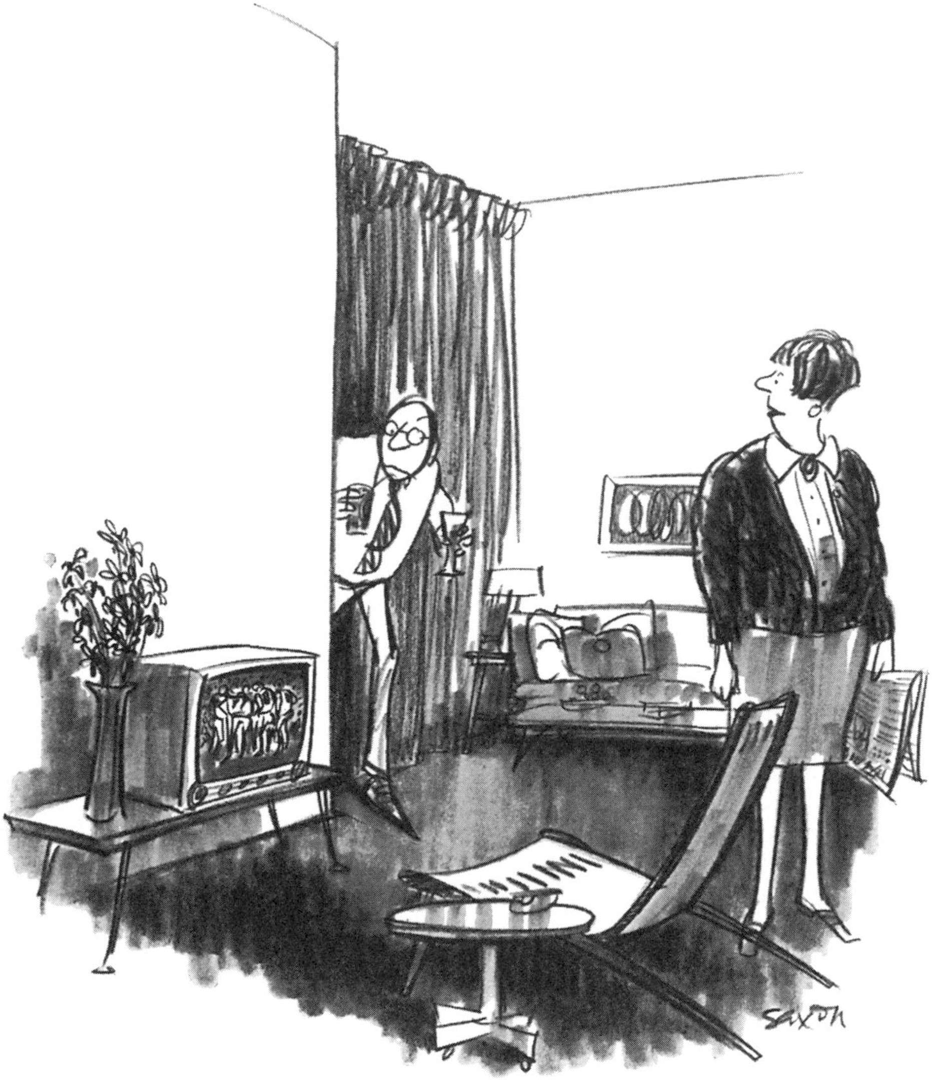
SAXON

"I think you just missed something. The ball went up in the air and somebody caught it and the crowd's yelling like mad."

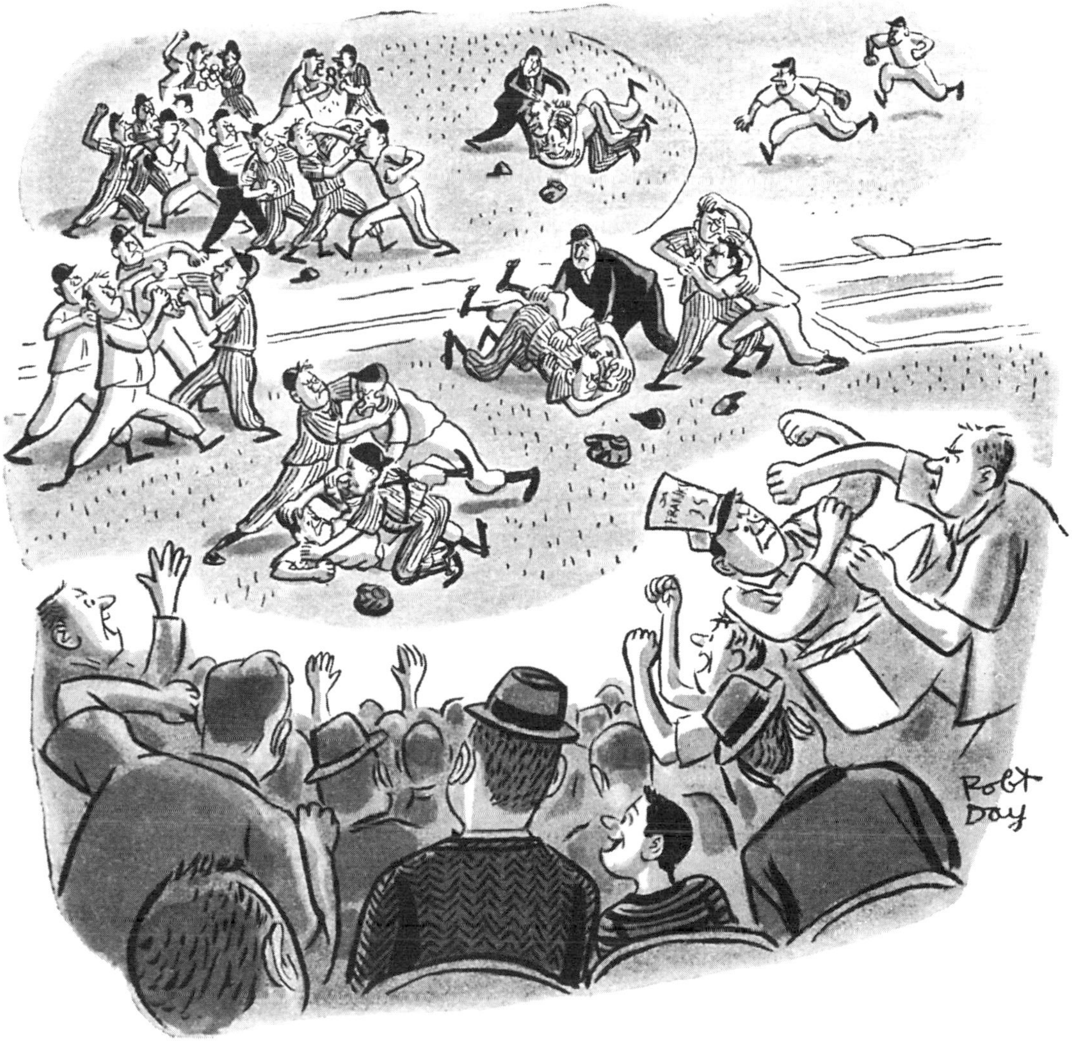
Robt
Day

"Gee, Dad, aren't you glad we came?"

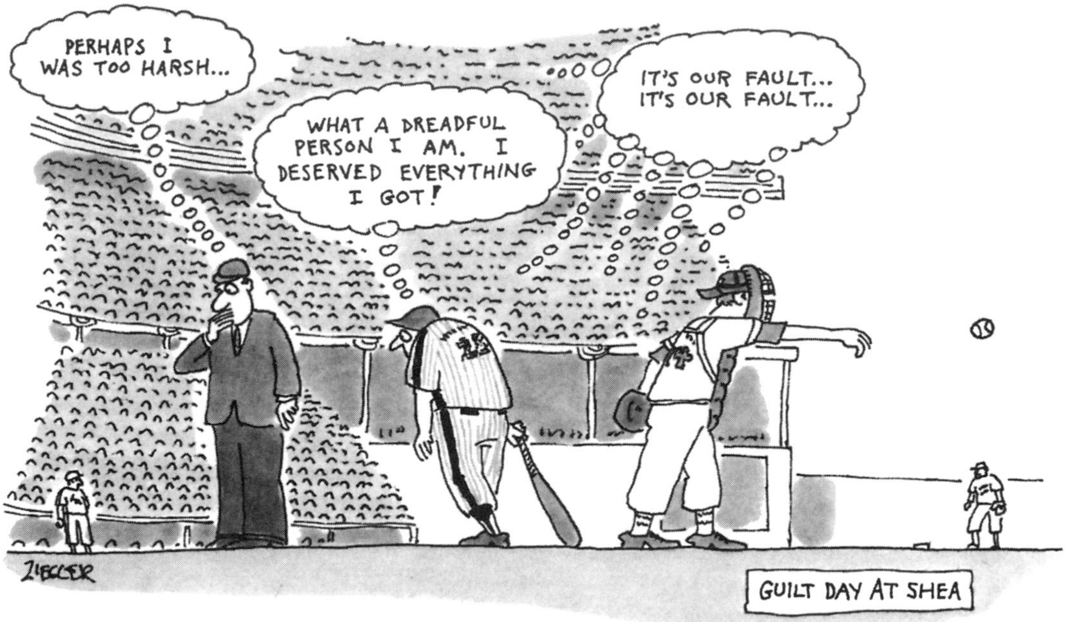
PERHAPS I WAS TOO HARSH...
WHAT A DREADFUL PERSON I AM. I DESERVED EVERYTHING I GOT!
IT'S OUR FAULT... IT'S OUR FAULT...
ZIEGLER
GUILT DAY AT SHEA

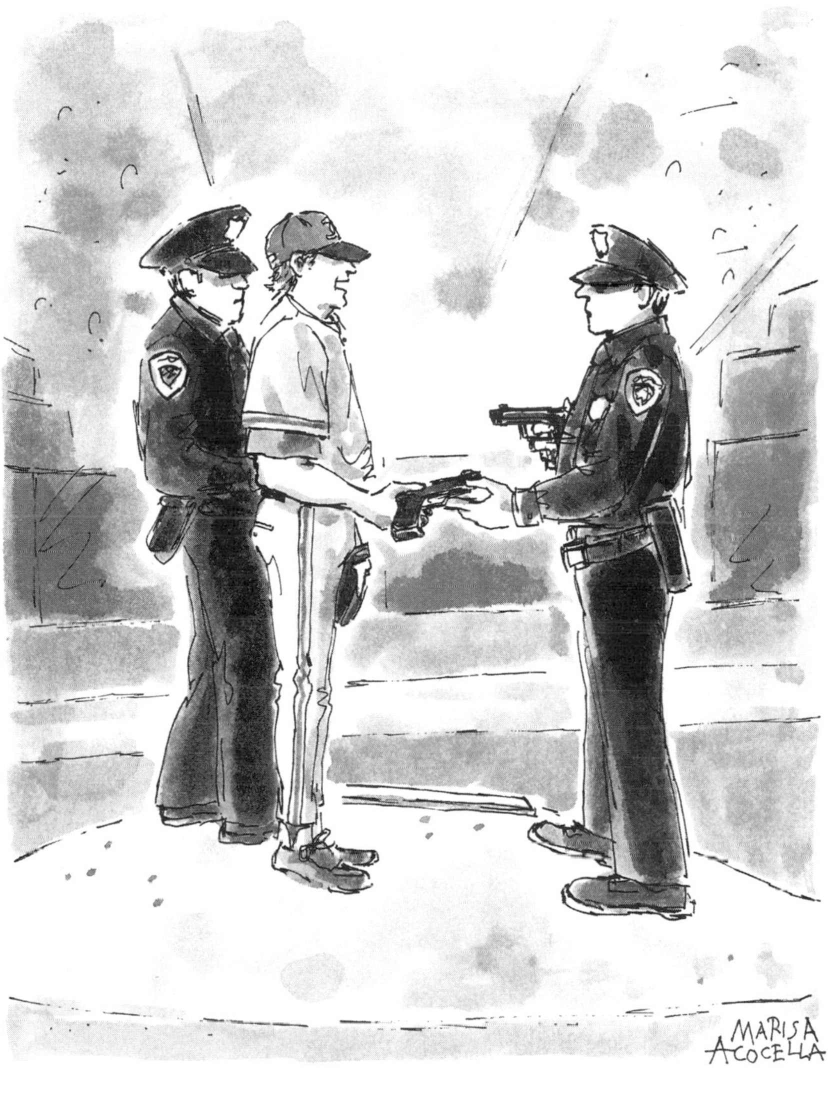
MARISA
ACOCELLA

"I was just trying to brush him back."

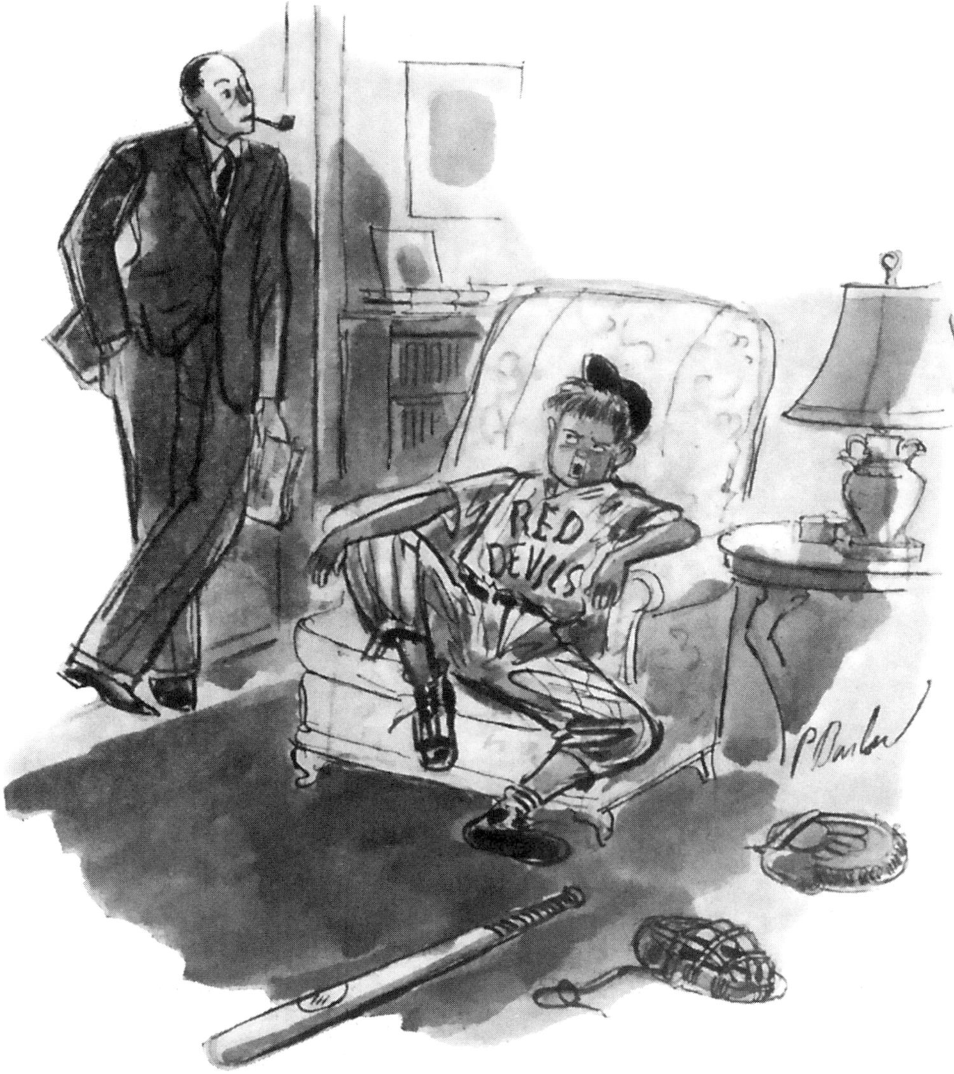
RED DEVILS

"Well—it was ten to three, favor of the girls."

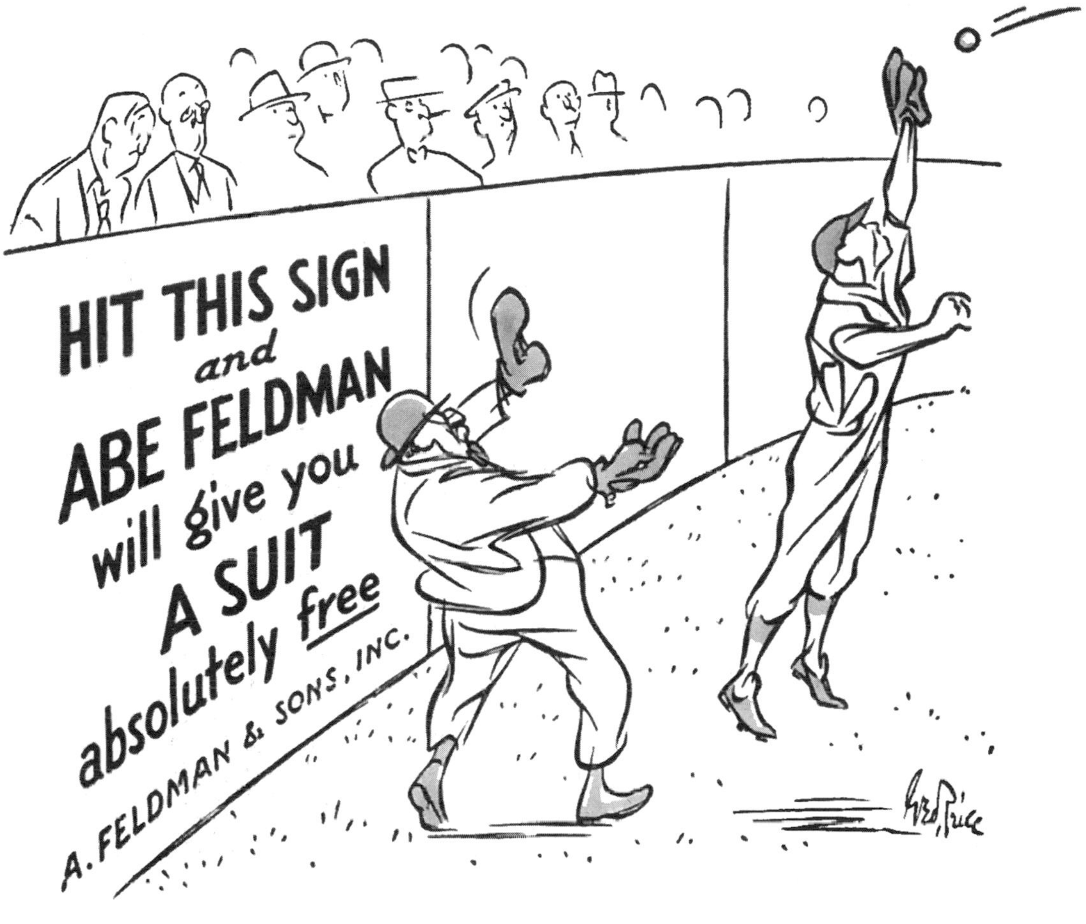
HIT THIS SIGN
and
ABE FELDMAN
will give you
A SUIT
absolutely free
A. FELDMAN & SONS, INC.
Fred Price

"Mr. Reynolds can't go out to play until he wraps up the Walderson contract."

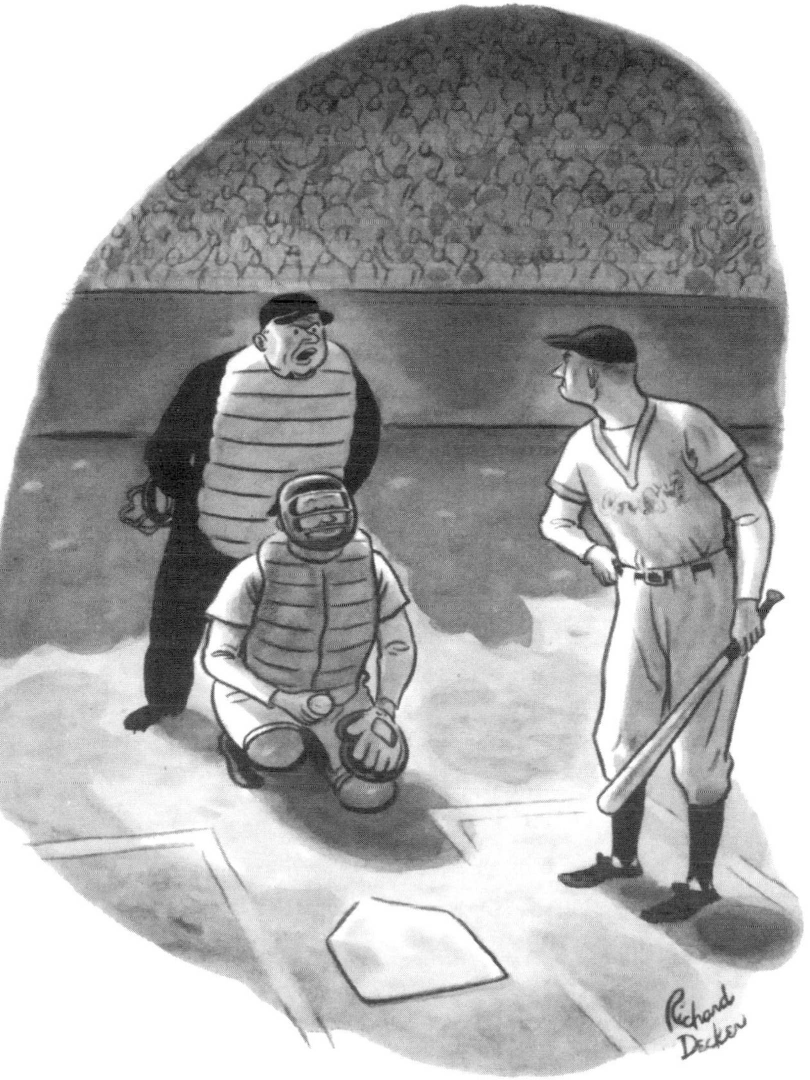
Richard Decker

"I don't think I'd say anything about eyesight if I had your batting average."

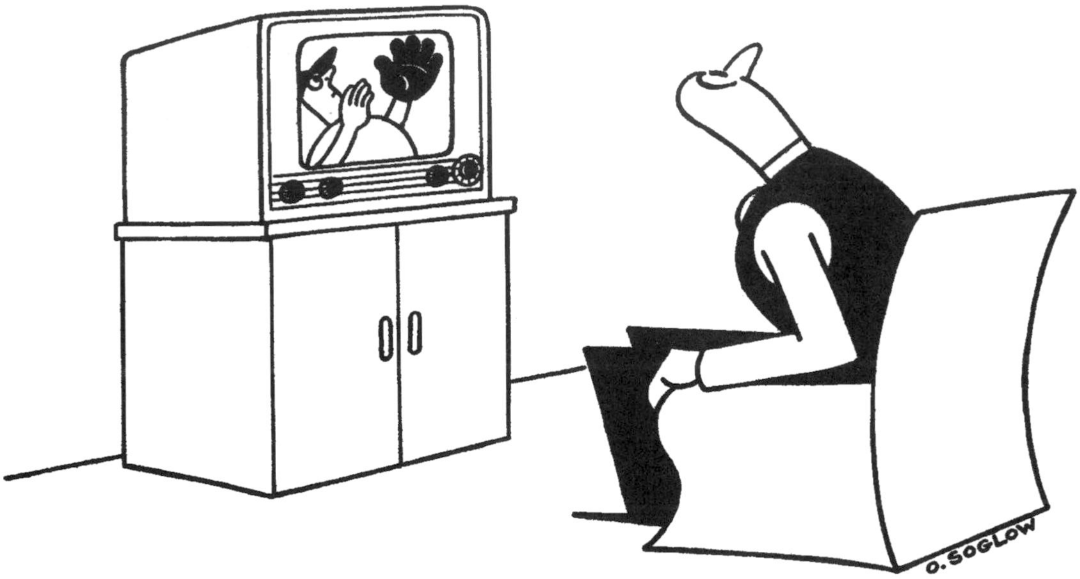
O. SOGLOW

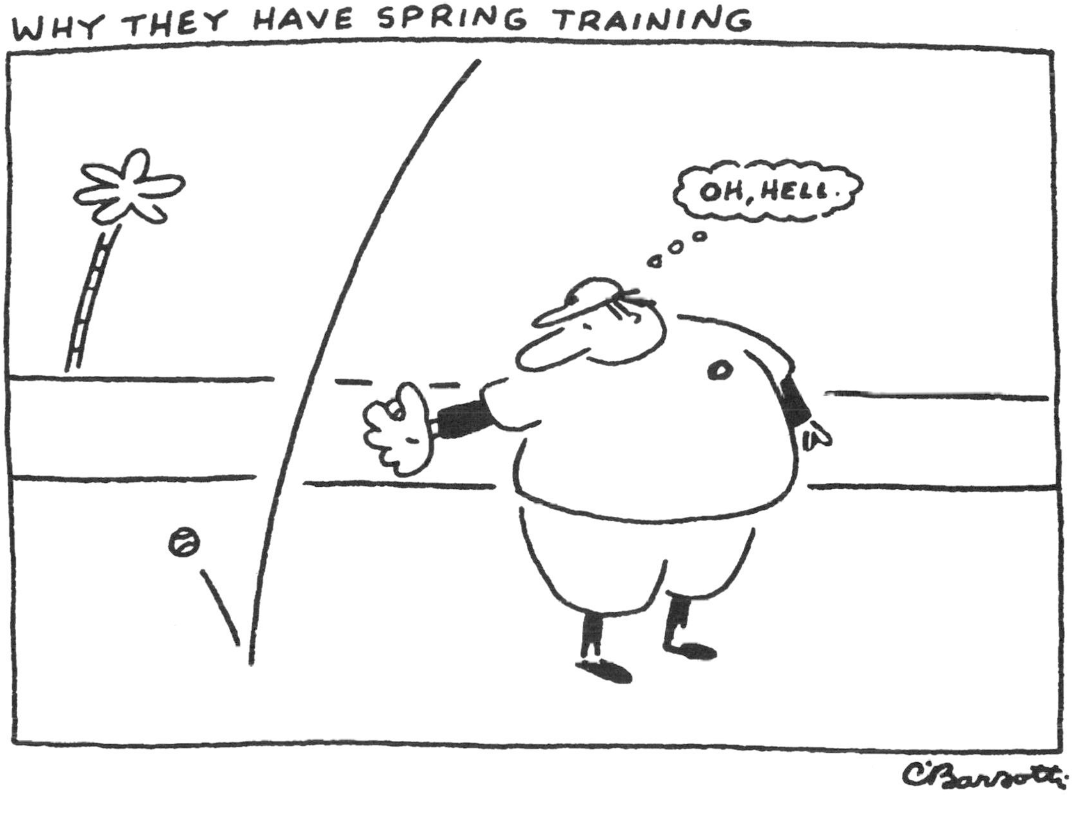
WHY THEY HAVE SPRING TRAINING
OH, HELL.

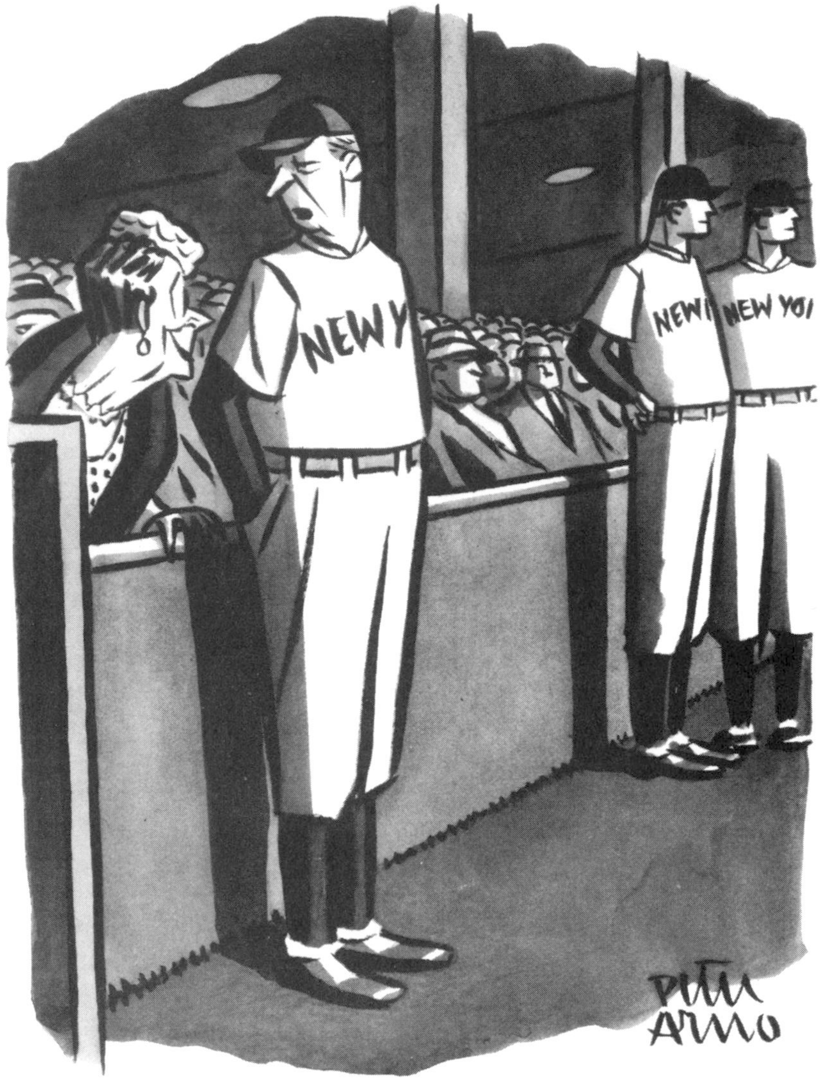
NEWY
NEWY
NEW YO

"Sometimes we sell them, lady, but only to other teams."

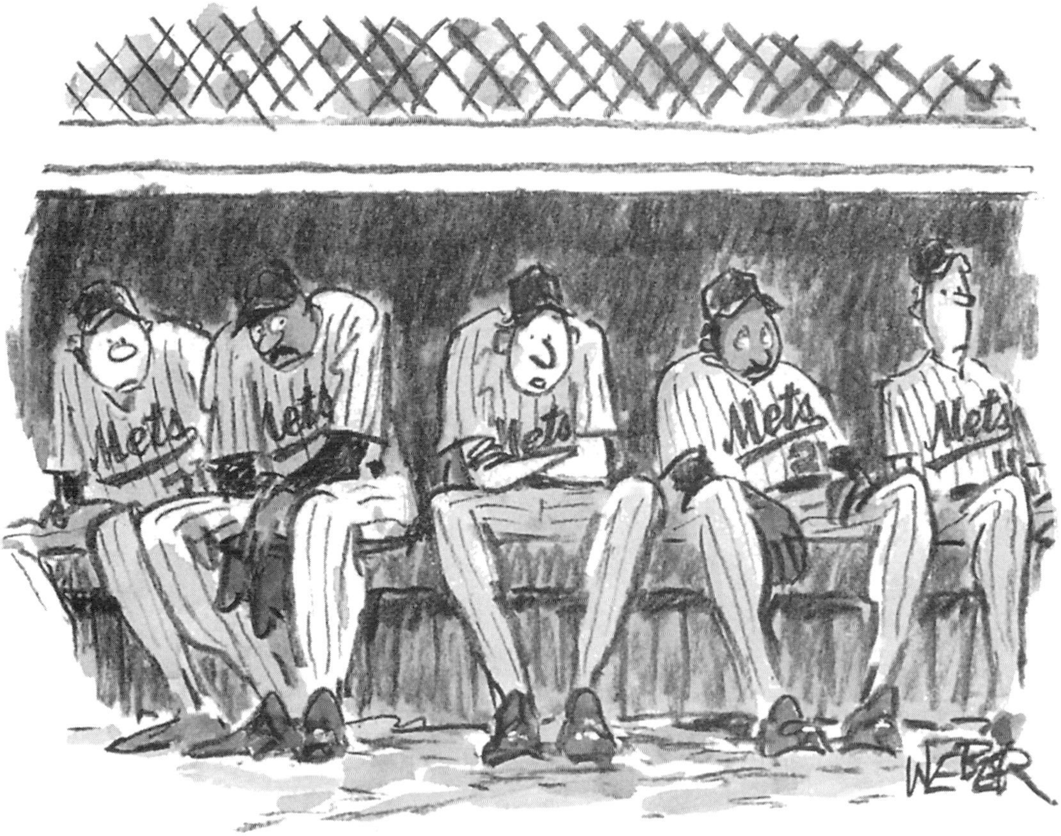
Mets
Mets
Mets
Mets
Mets
WEBER

"Maybe we weren't meant to express ourselves in this particular medium."

"*Your Honor, I have a rebuttal witness.*"

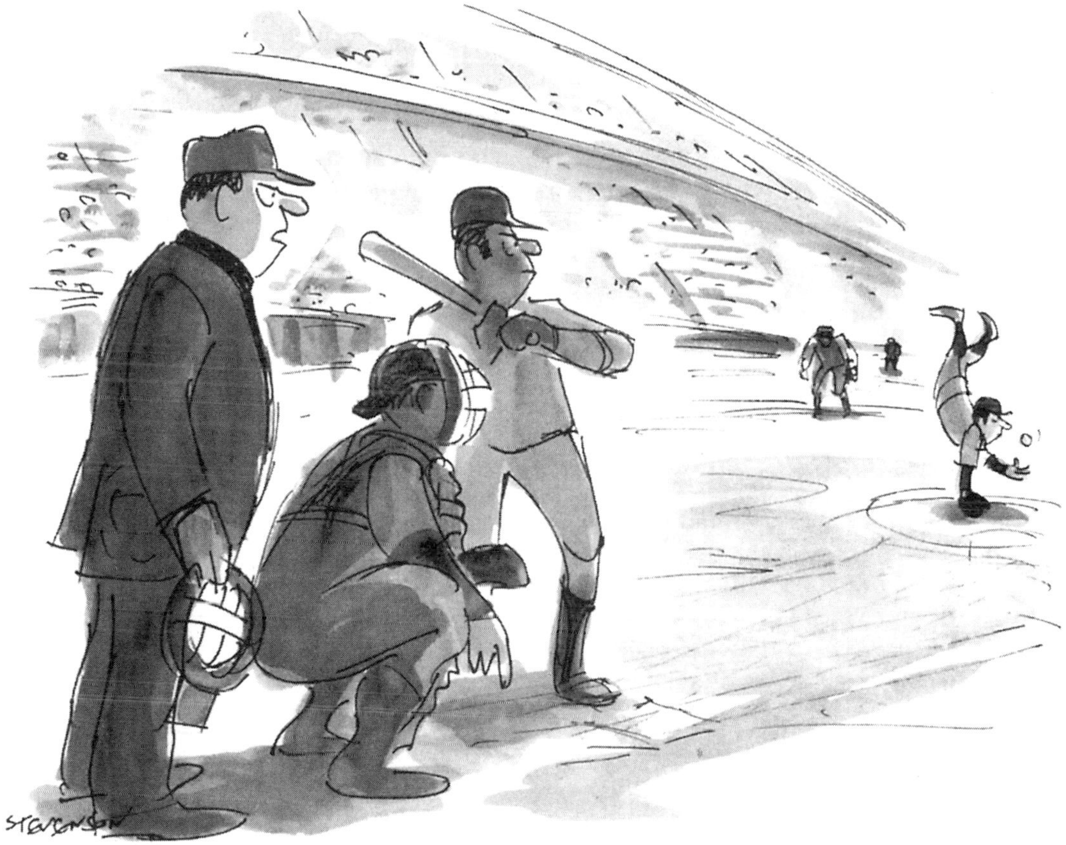
STEVENSON

"It may not be a balk, but it's something."

"We're offering twenty million plus incentives over a four-year period, Mrs. Morton. Can Timmy come out and play?"

"I've noticed this one before. He seems to be _very_ tidy."

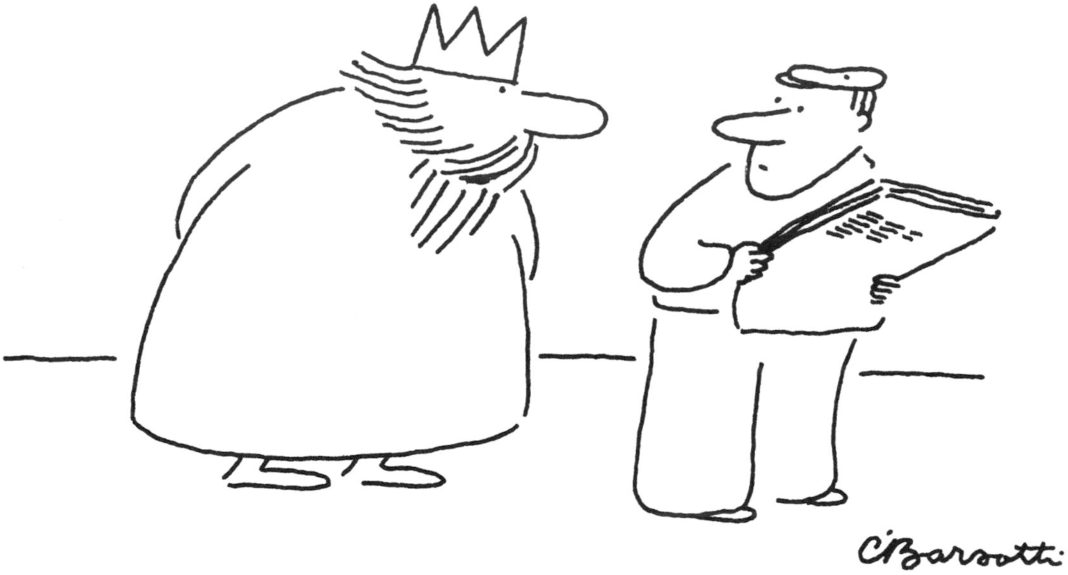
CBarsotti

"How are the Royals doing?"

WHY THE BALL IS JUMPING OUT

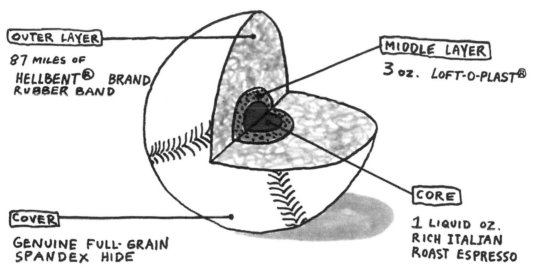

OUTER LAYER

87 MILES OF HELLBENT® BRAND RUBBER BAND

MIDDLE LAYER

3 OZ. LOFT-O-PLAST®

CORE

1 LIQUID OZ. RICH ITALIAN ROAST ESPRESSO

COVER

GENUINE FULL-GRAIN SPANDEX HIDE

CRAWFORD

"My trouble is—by the time I get warmed up, I'm all pooped out."

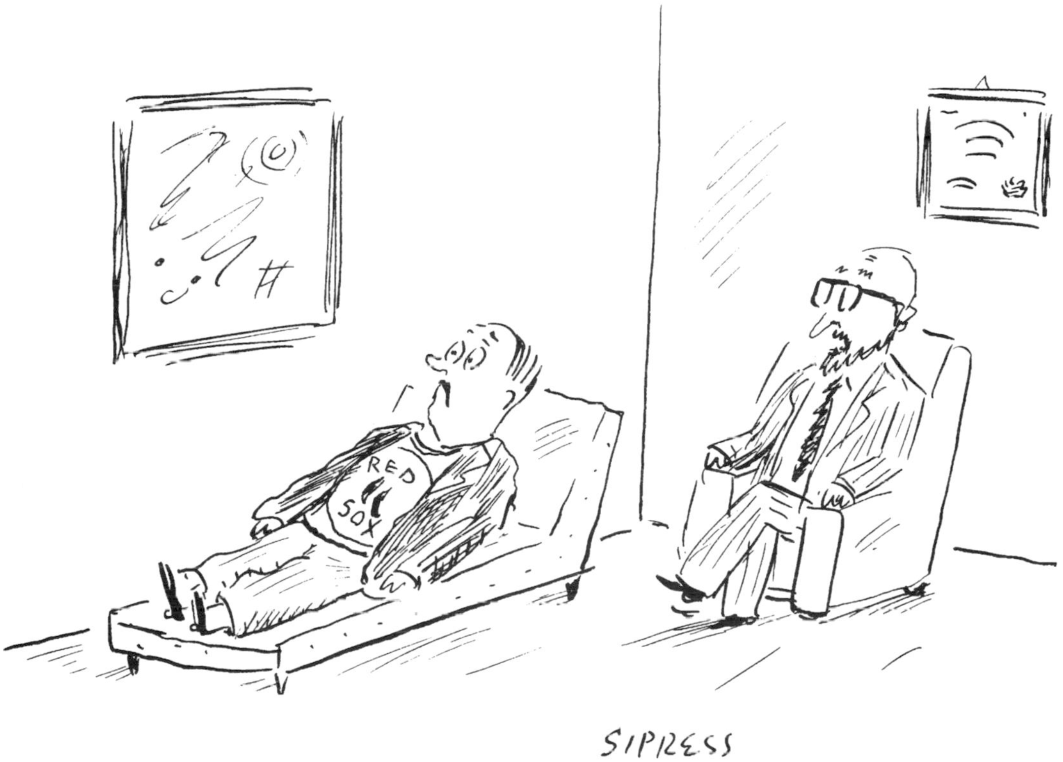
RED SOX
SIPRESS

"Rooting for them is a disease, Ben. It's nothing to be ashamed of."

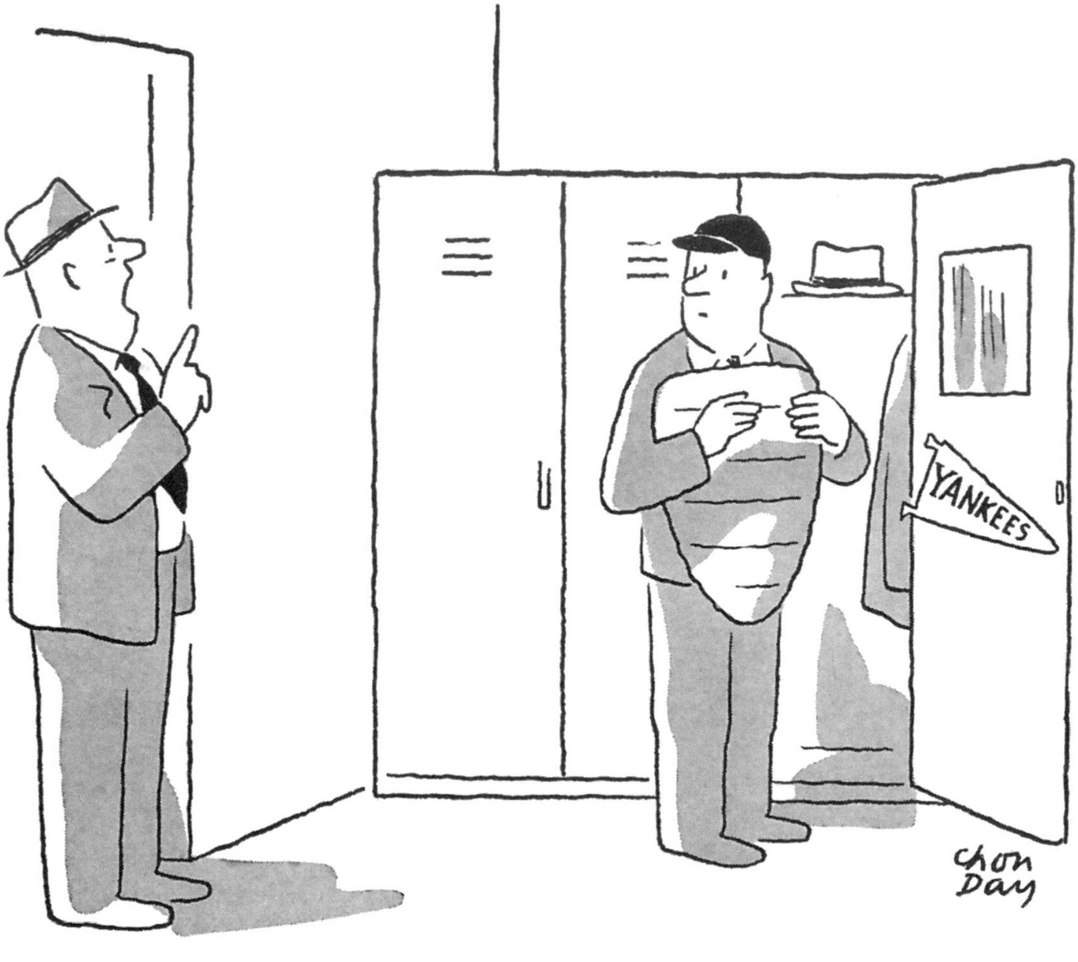
YANKEES
chon Day

"Oh, Harris, I'd like a word with you."

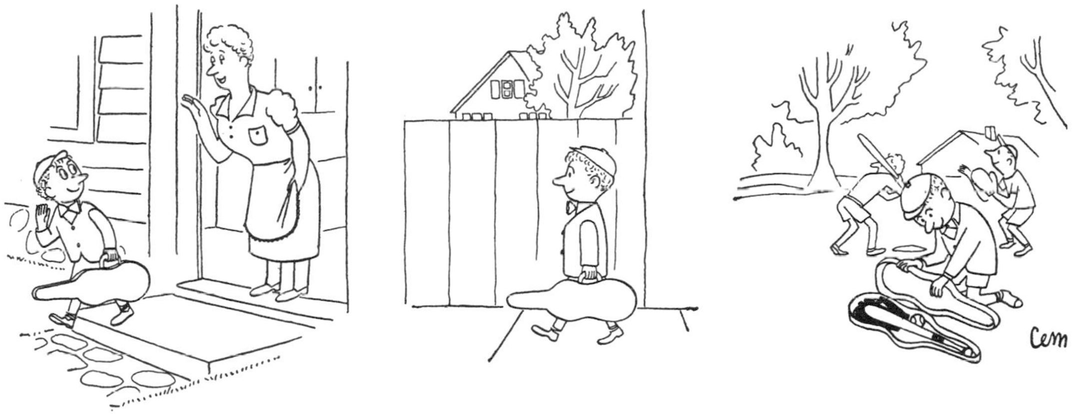
Cem

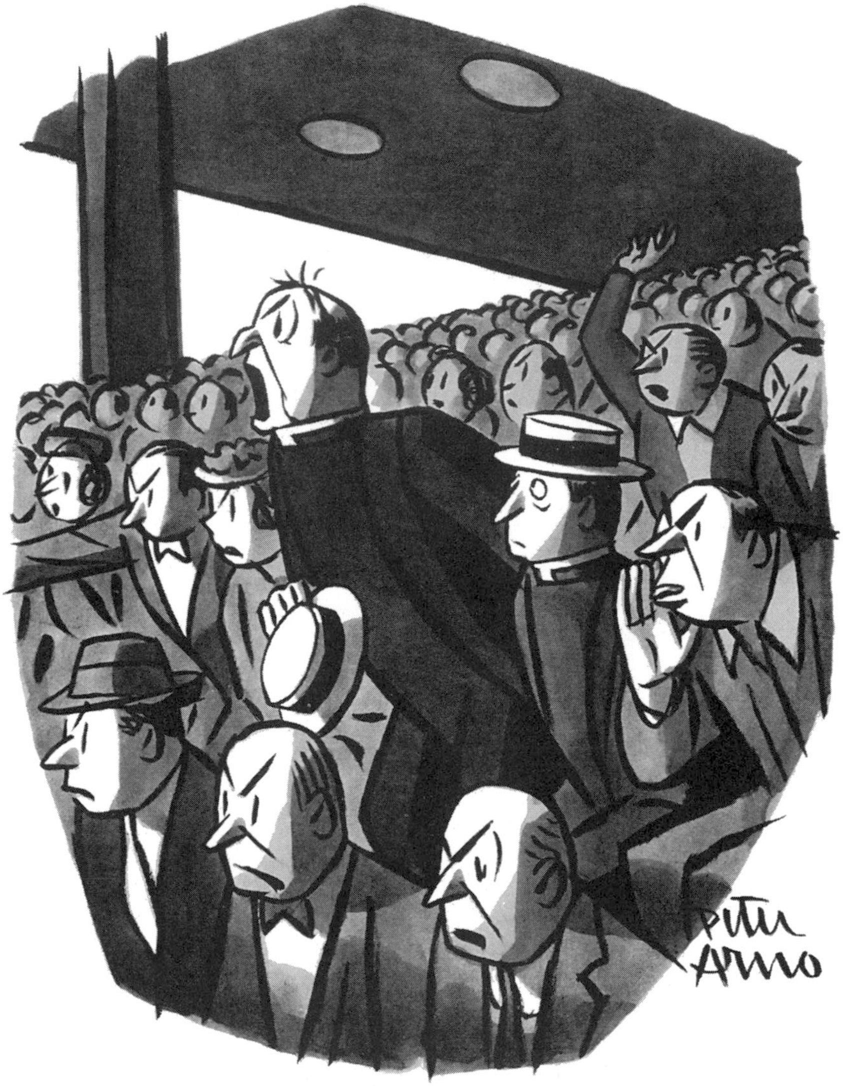
Peter Arno

"Thou hast eyes to see, and see not!"

"I __am__ standing up straight!"

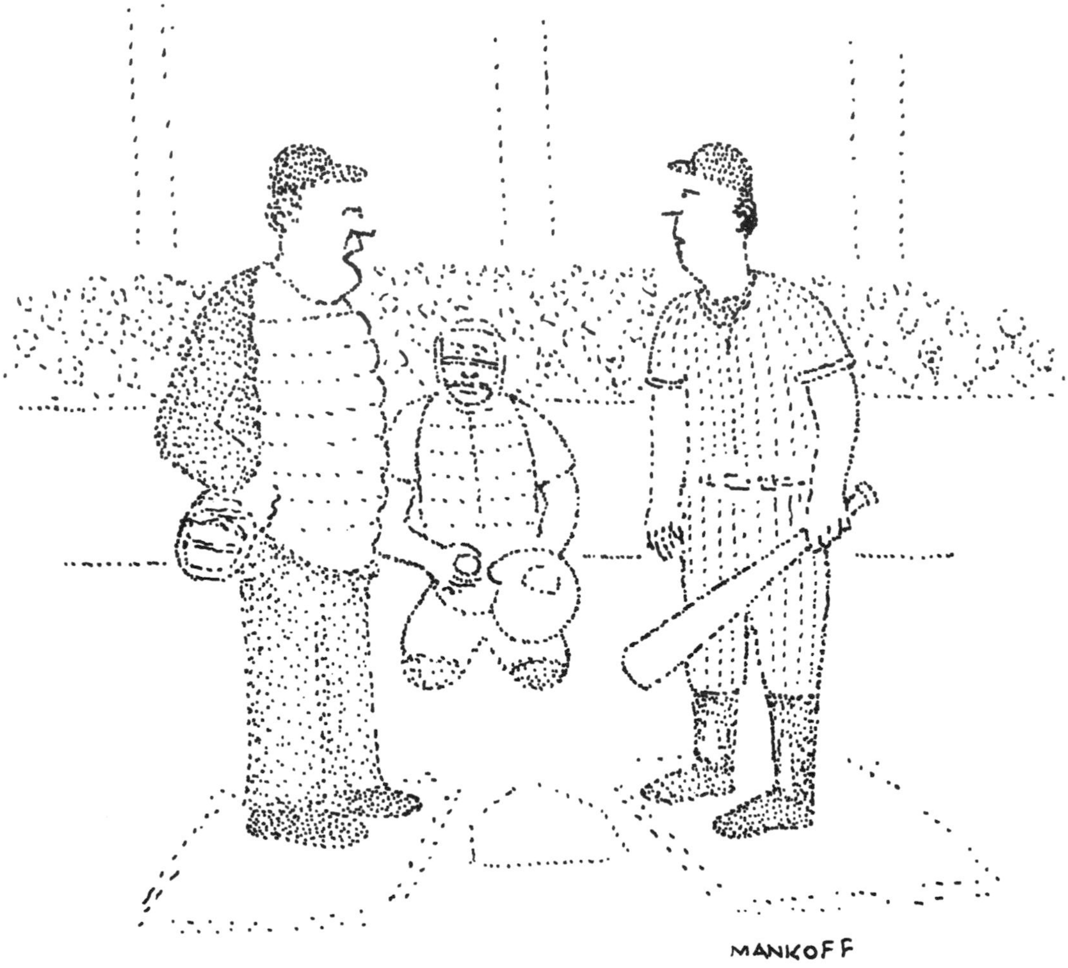
MANKOFF

"All right! Have it your own way. It was a ball."

"I see we're not wearing our Mets cap."

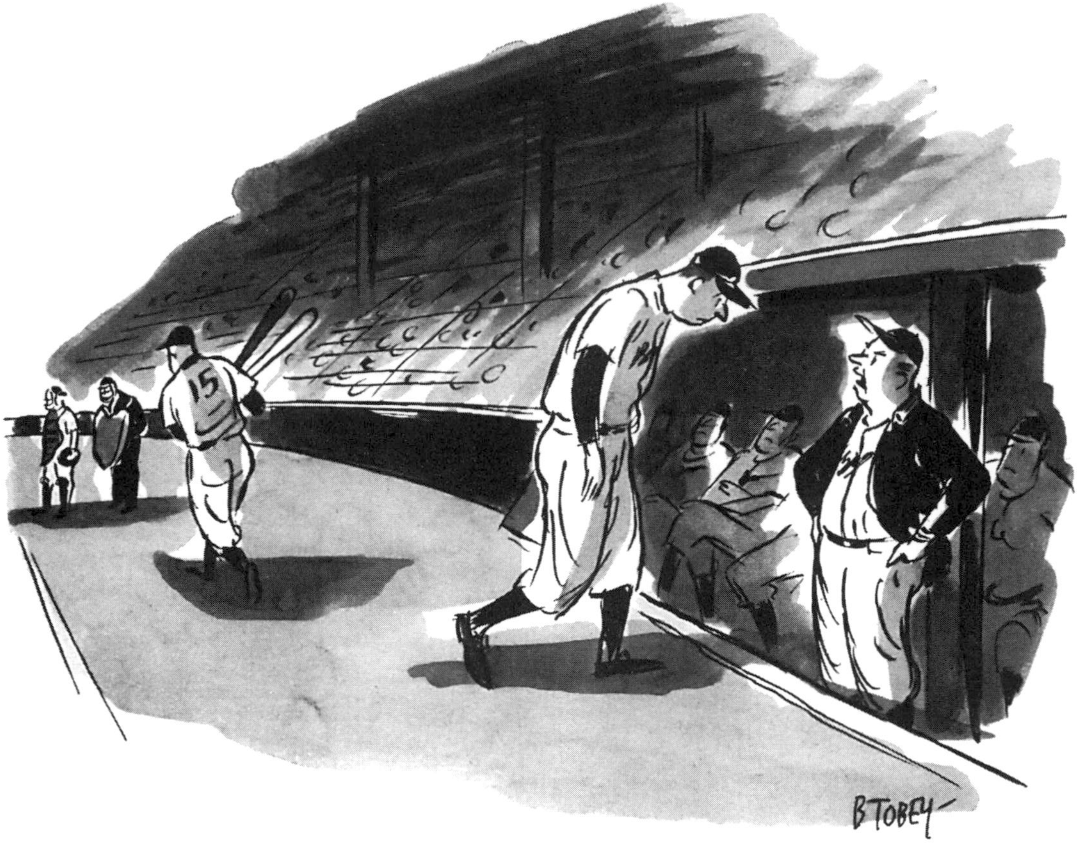
15
B TOBEY

"You had me worried. For one horrible moment I thought you were going to slide and soil your uniform."

"All I seem to have brought with me is
a headful of baseball statistics."

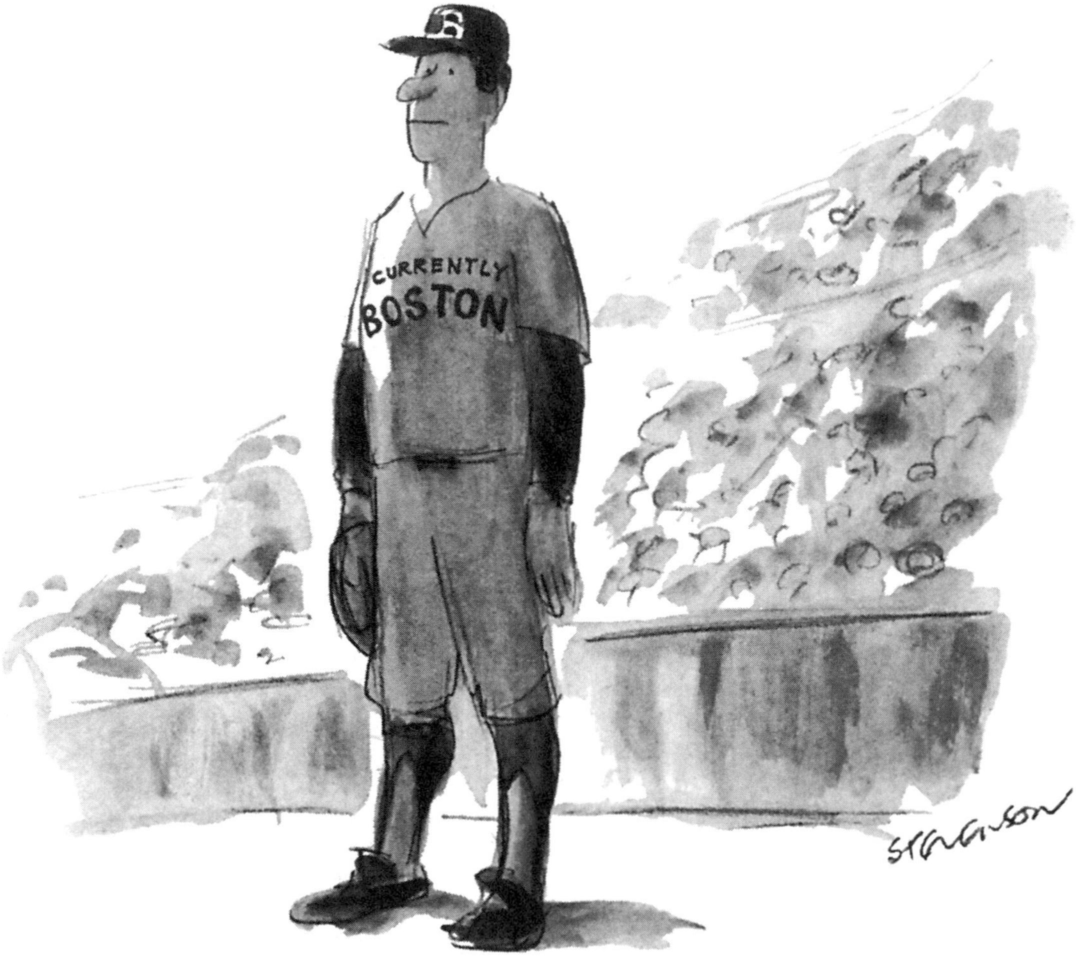
CURRENTLY
BOSTON
STEVENSON

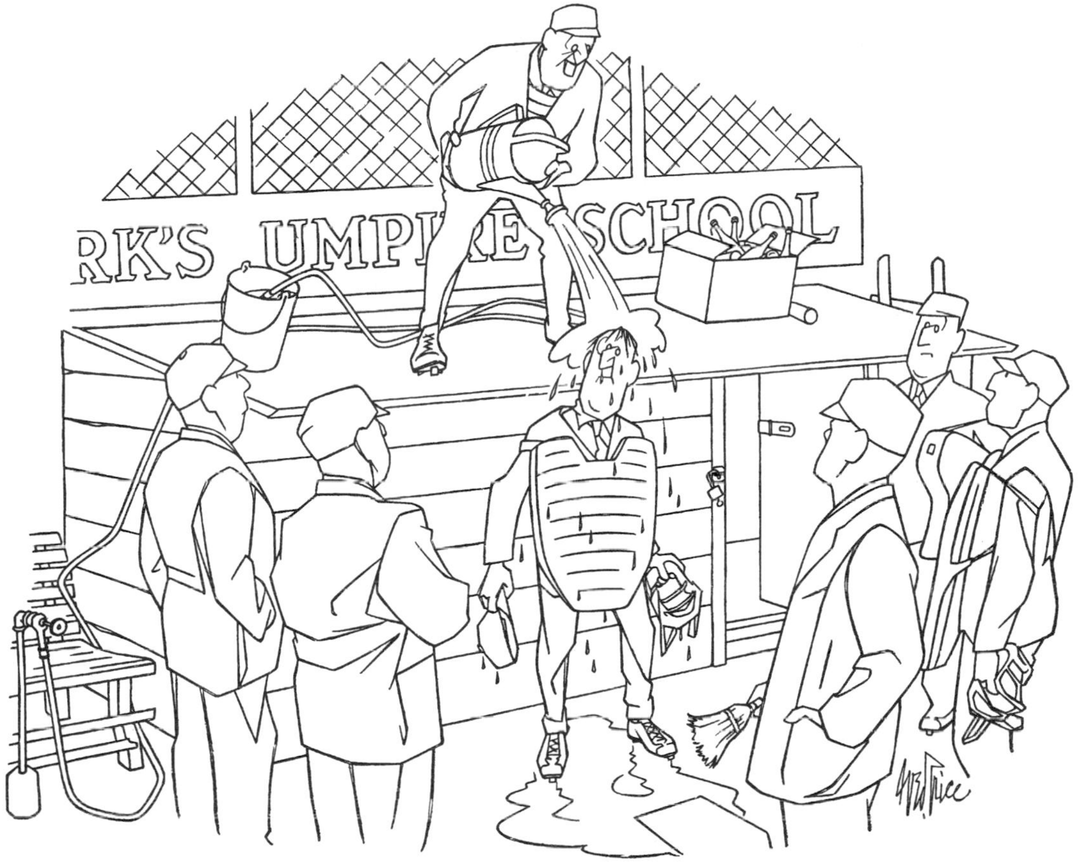
RK'S UMP RE SCHOOL

"All right, it's starting to come down a little heavier. Now would you call the game?"

R.J.D.

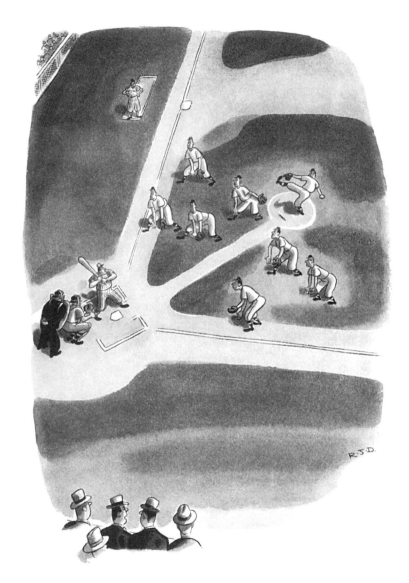

"They expect him to bunt."

"You always rush out and high-five me when I
homer. How 'bout a hug when I whiff?"

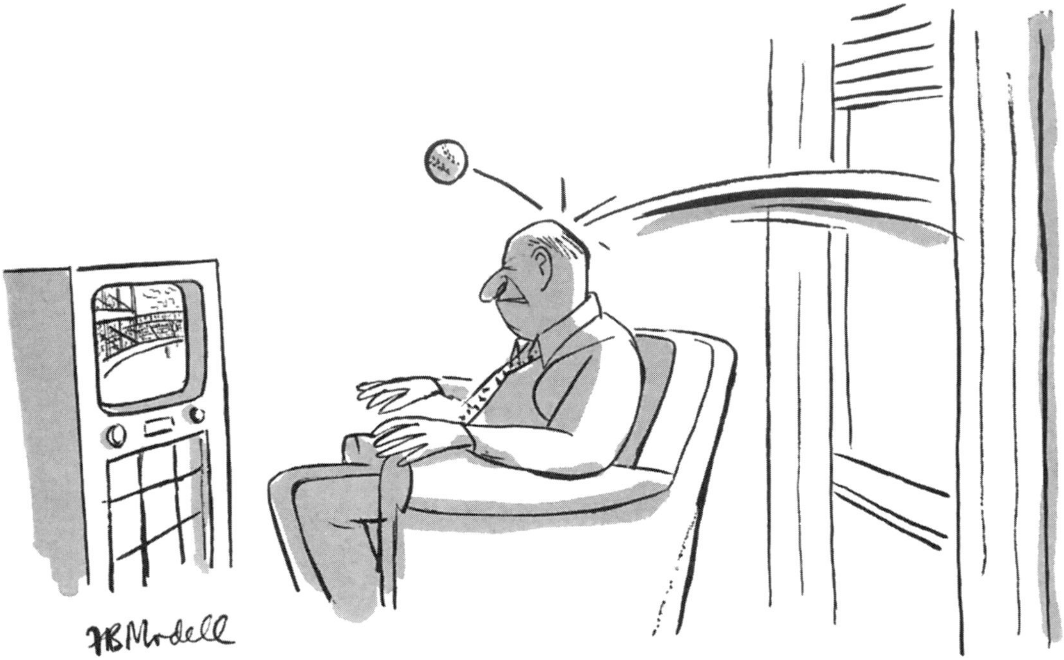
FBModell

"There it goes, folks, high over center field and still travelling. It looks like—Yes, sir, it is! It's bye-bye, baby!"

"This game isn't being televised, O'Malley. A simple 'Out' would have sufficed."

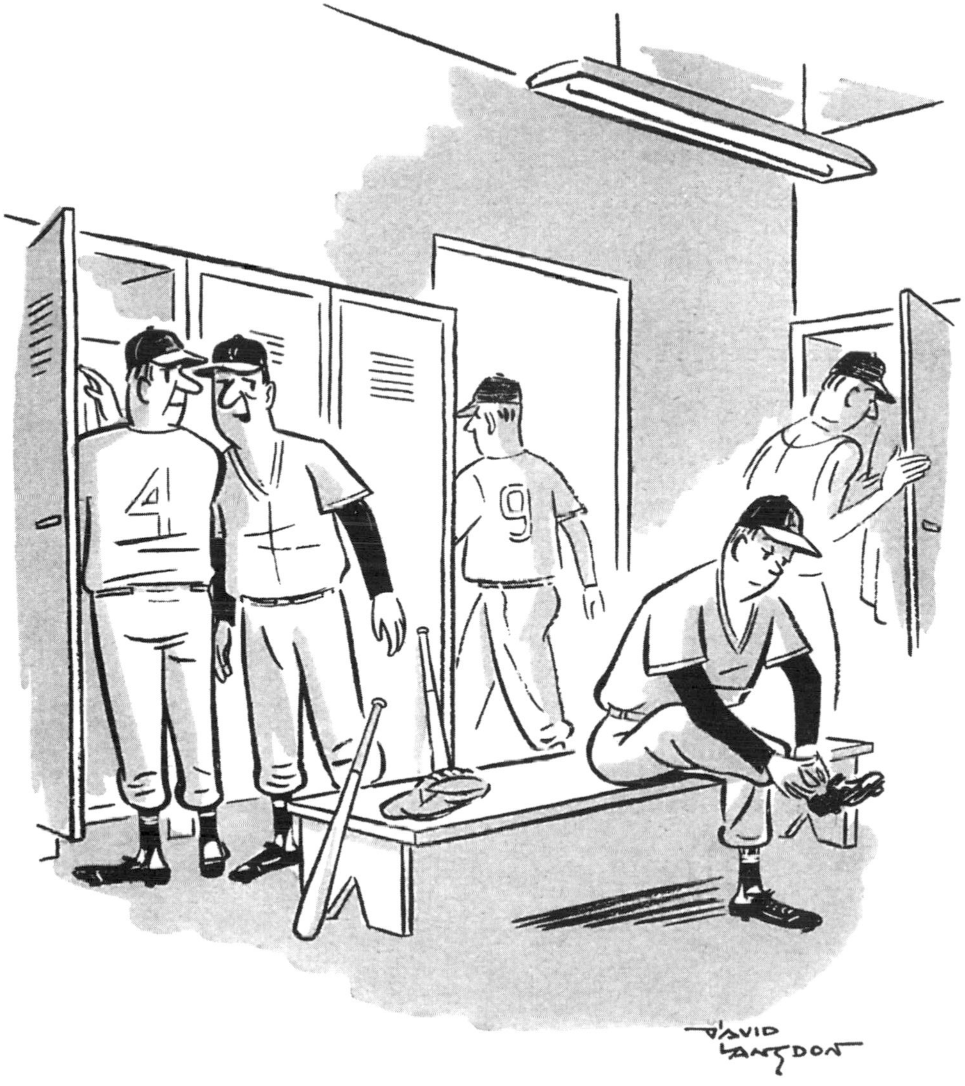
DAVID LANGDON

"Tough break for the kid! Gillette had him all lined up for an endorsement until they found out he doesn't shave."

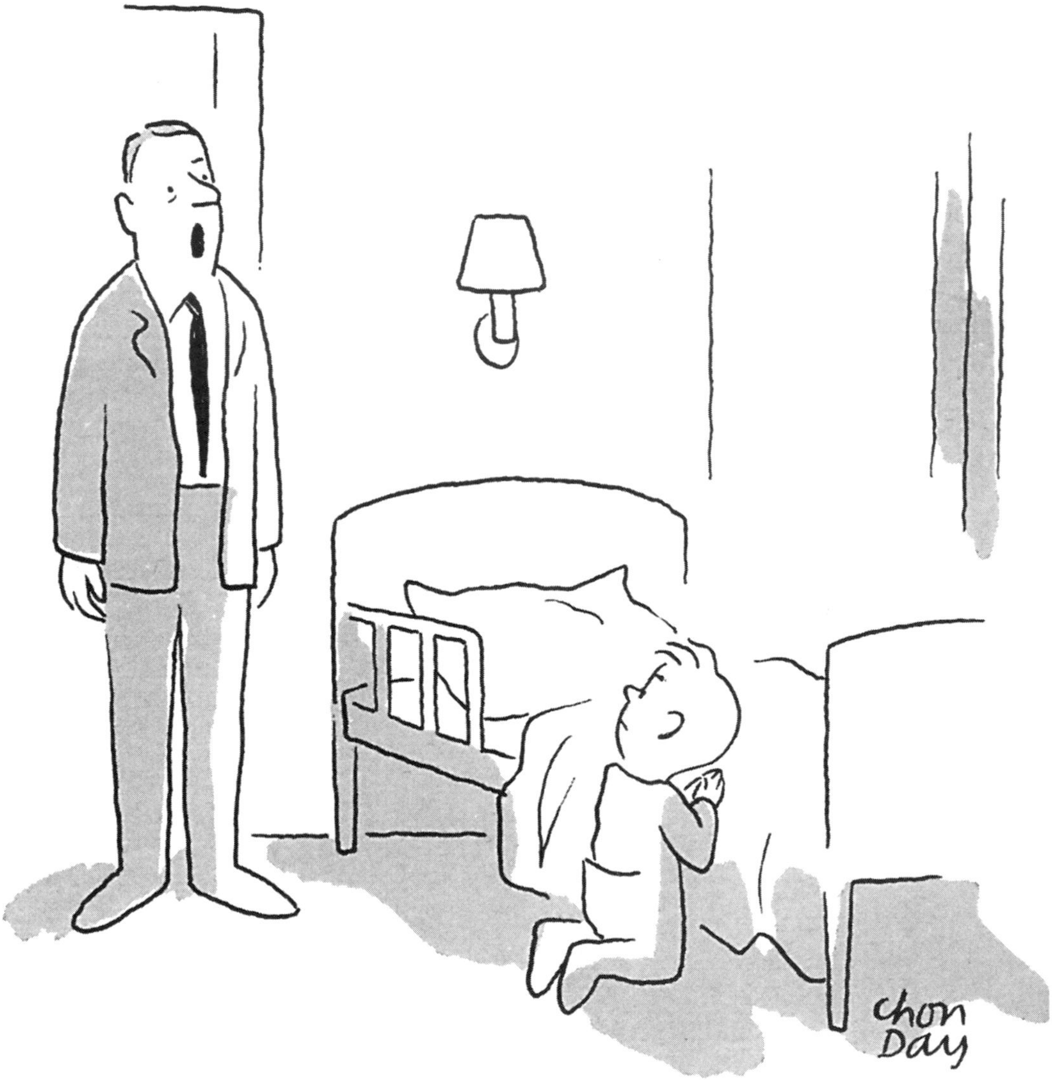
chon
Day

"Never mind mentioning all twenty-five of them. Just 'God bless the Mets' will do."

"The game's gotten too damn big-business, if you ask me."

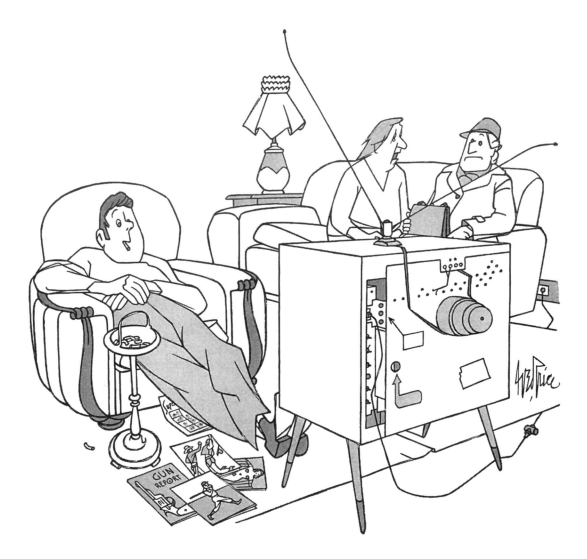

"*Success came too early. When he was ten, he hit three homers in three times up in the Little League, and nothing has seemed worthwhile since.*"

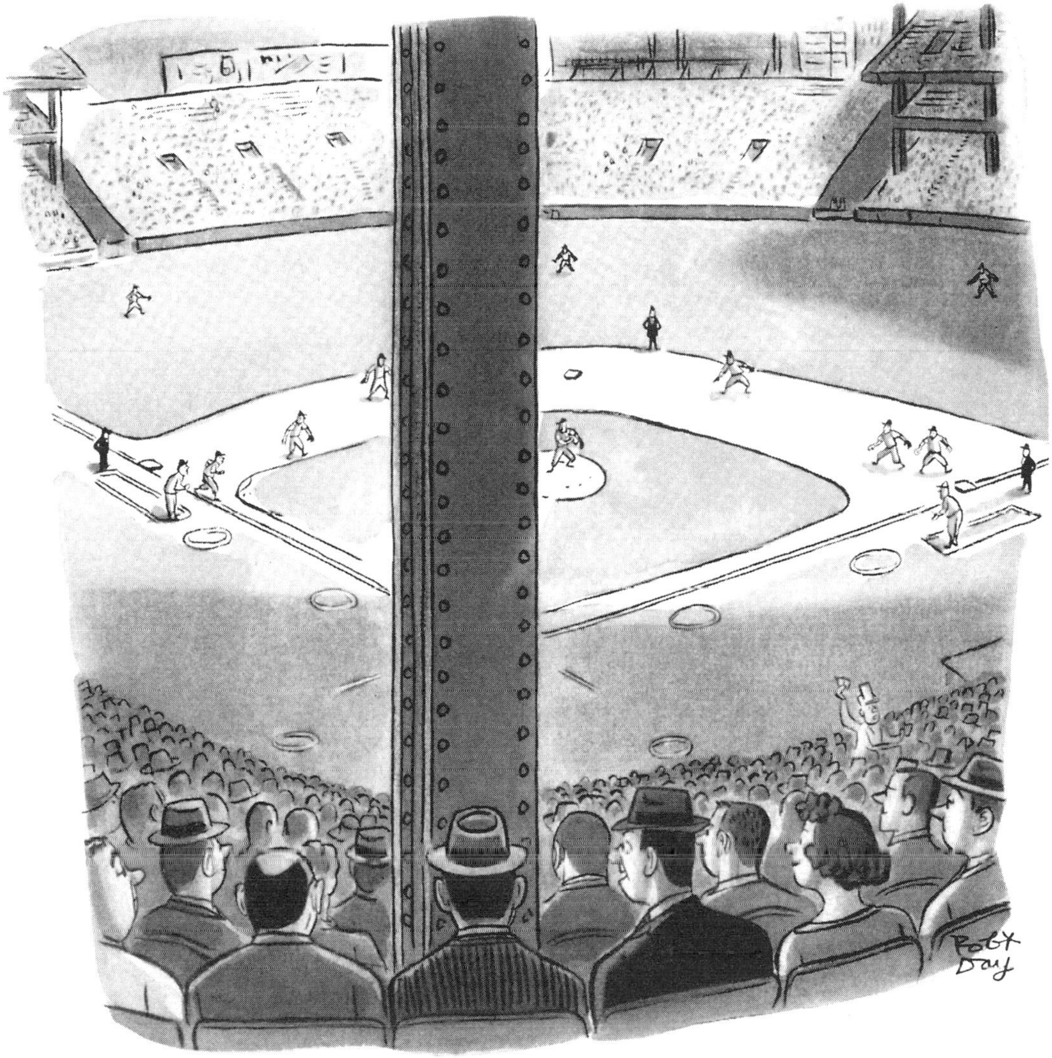
Robt
Day

"High inside. Ball three. Count is now three balls and two strikes. Here comes the pitch."

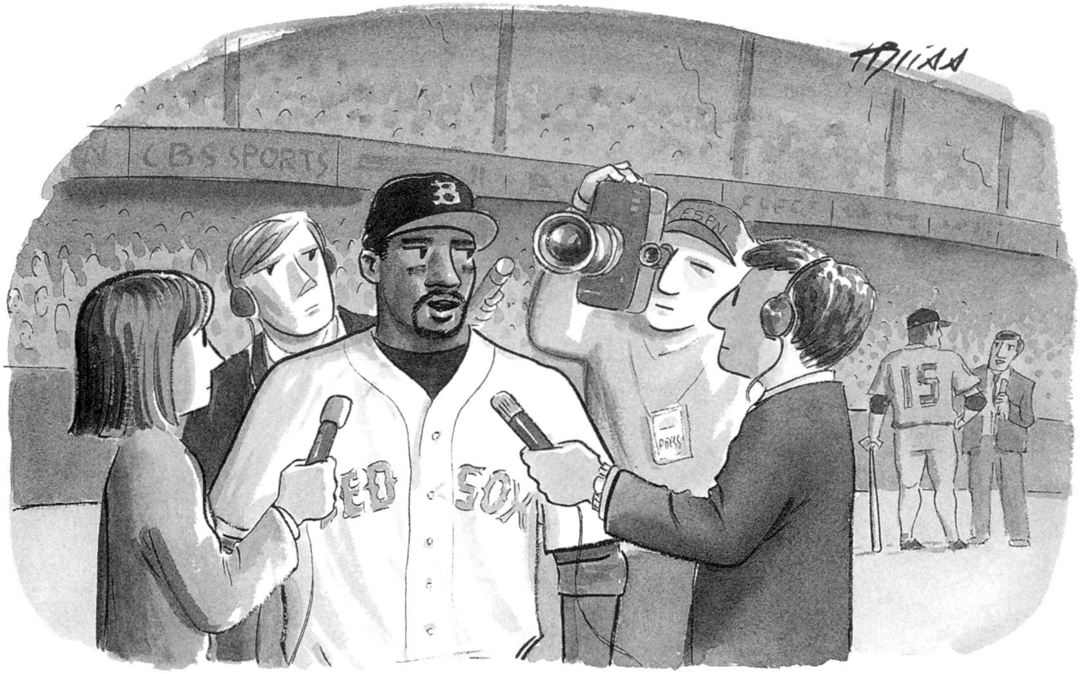
CBS SPORTS
ESPN
RED SOX
15
PRESS

"Hey, I'm just happy to be making an obscene amount of money."

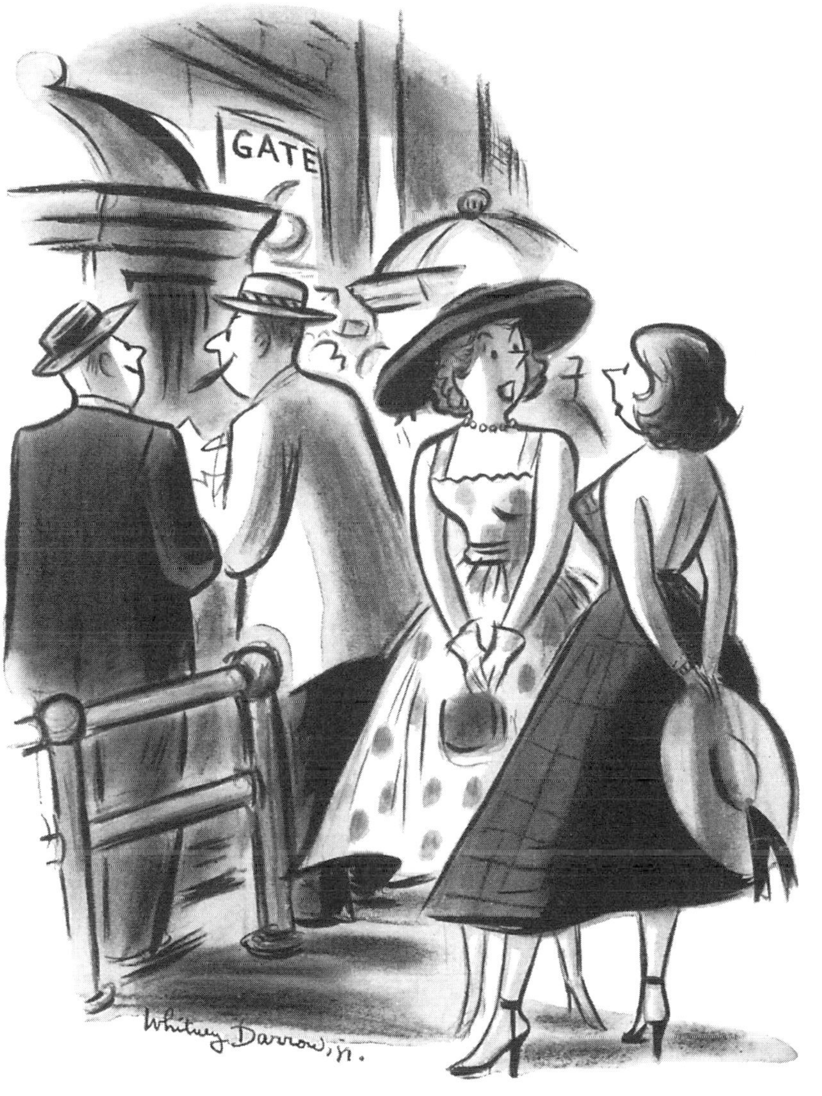
GATE
Whitney Darrow, Jr.

"I'll be glad when Bill and I are married and I can stop pretending I don't know anything about baseball."

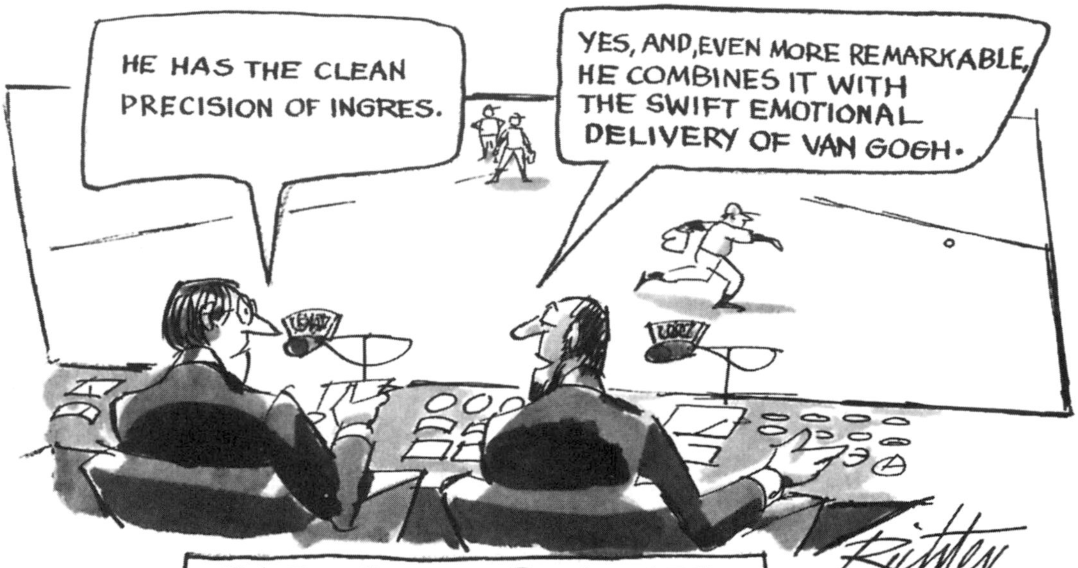
HE HAS THE CLEAN PRECISION OF INGRES.
YES, AND, EVEN MORE REMARKABLE, HE COMBINES IT WITH THE SWIFT EMOTIONAL DELIVERY OF VAN GOGH.
Richter

BASEBALL REACHES FOR THE PBS AUDIENCE.

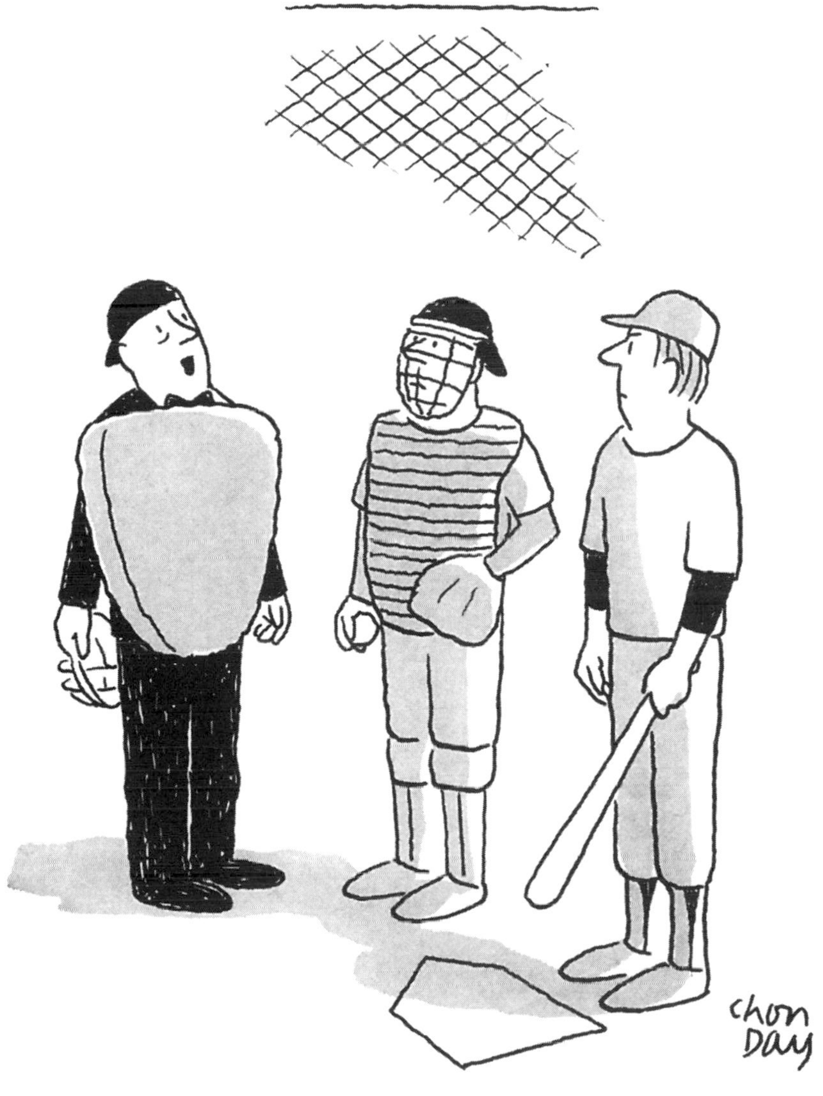
Chon Day

"I'm sorry, but I wasn't really paying attention."

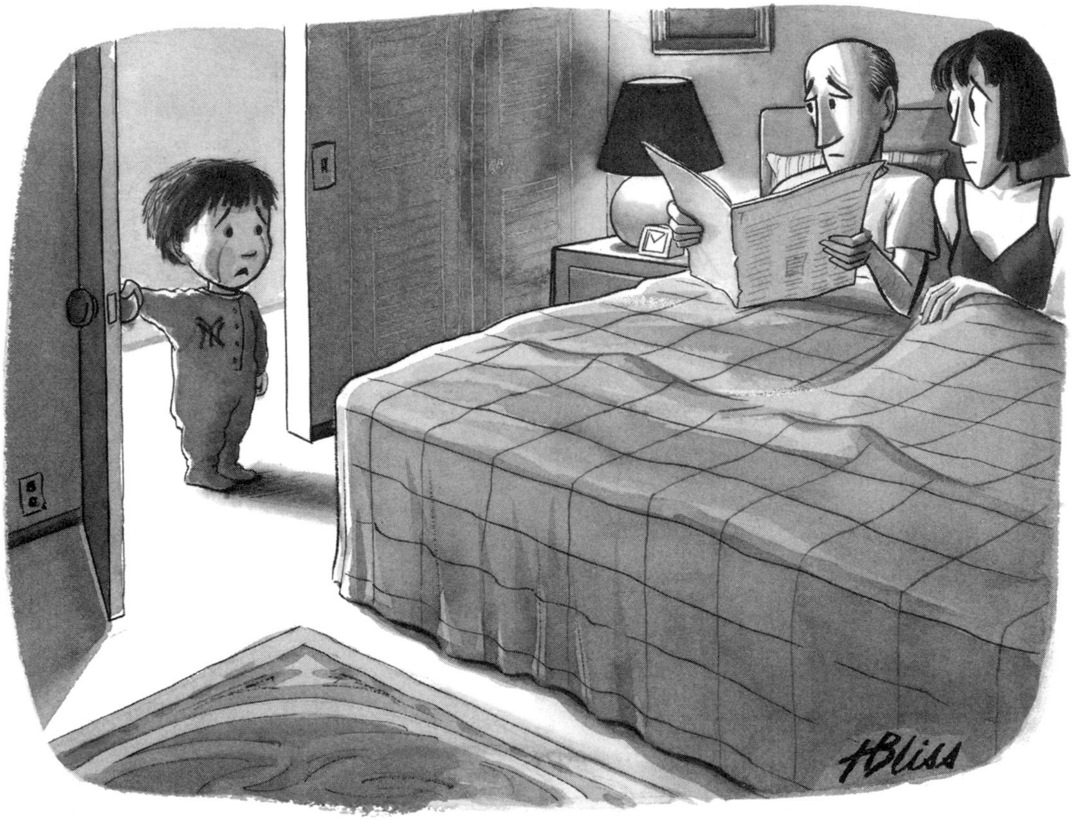
H Bliss

"I dreamed the Yankees lost in Game Seven."

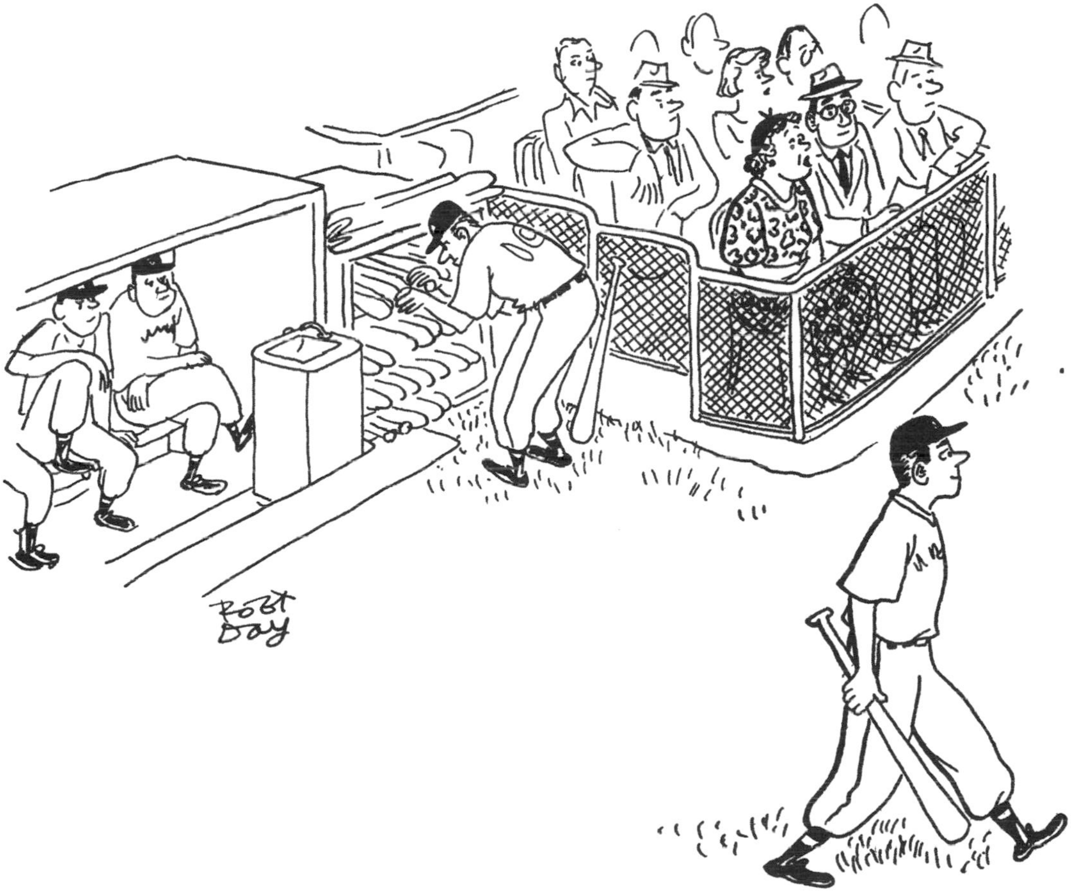
ROBT DAY

"Well, he doesn't look like any two hundred thousand dollars to me."

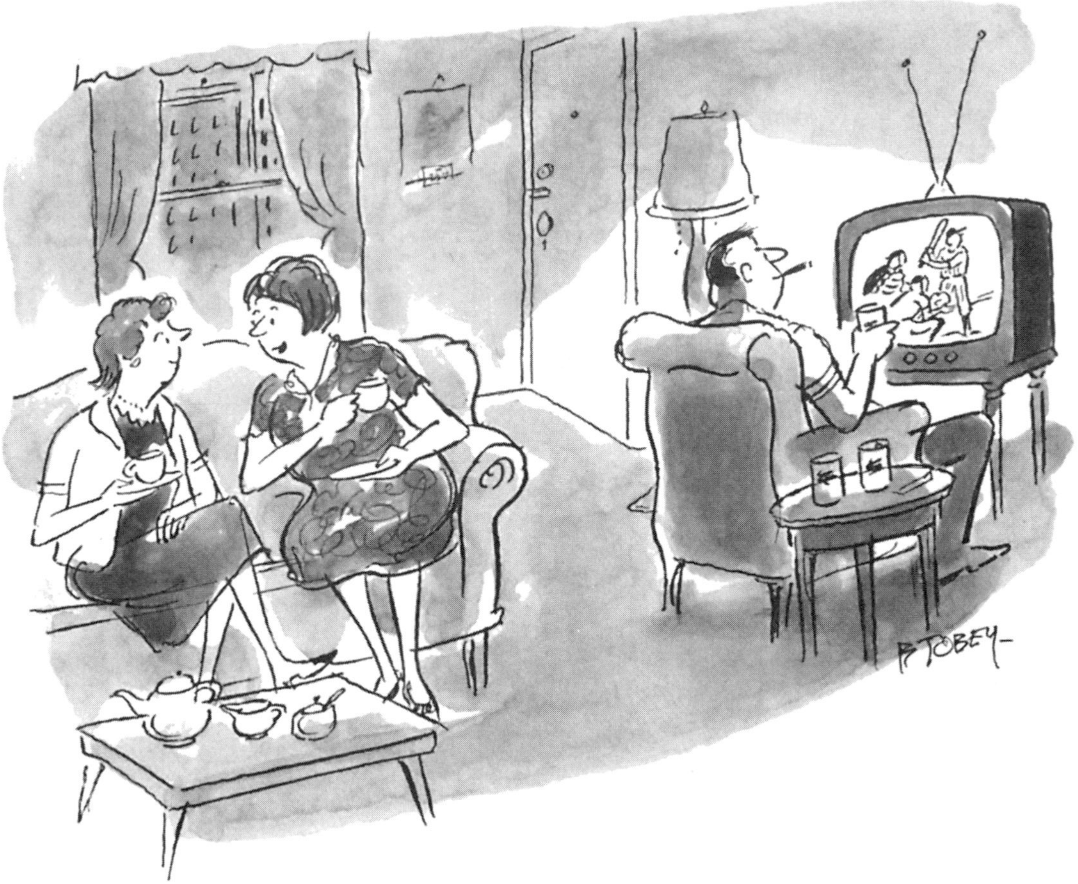
B. TOBEY

"From now until October, he'll be quiet as a pussycat."

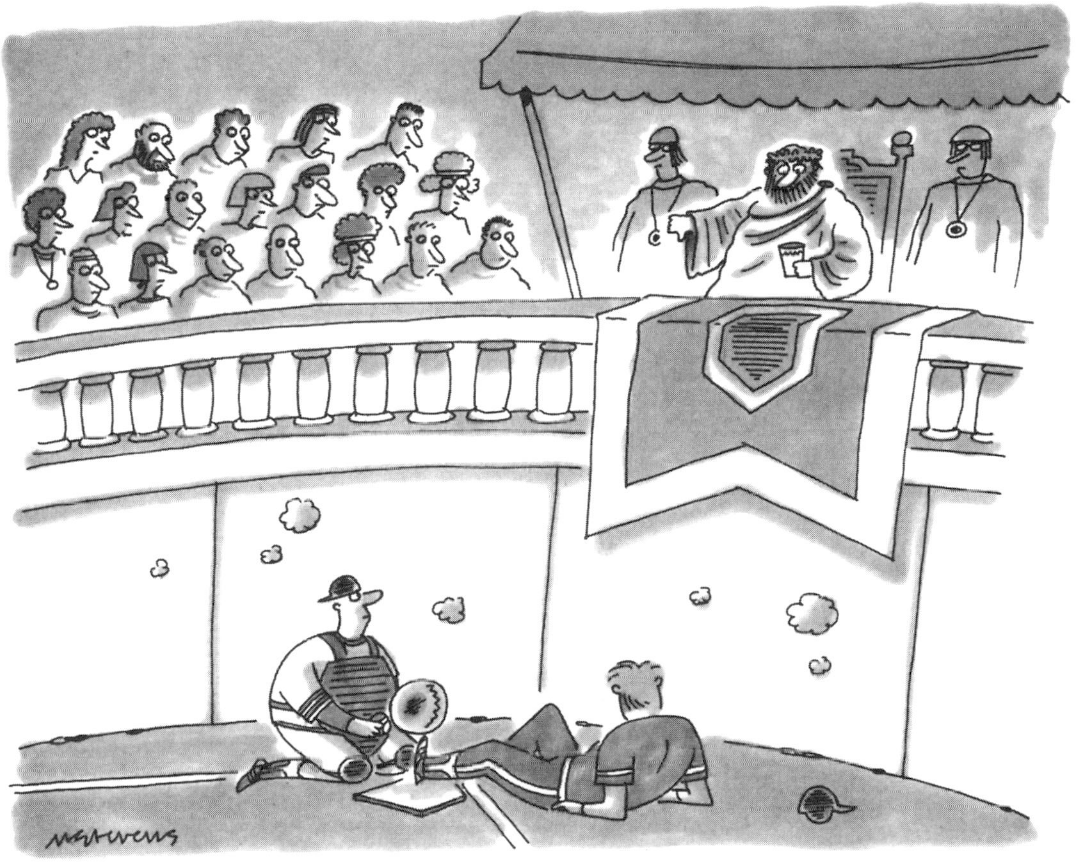
MStevens

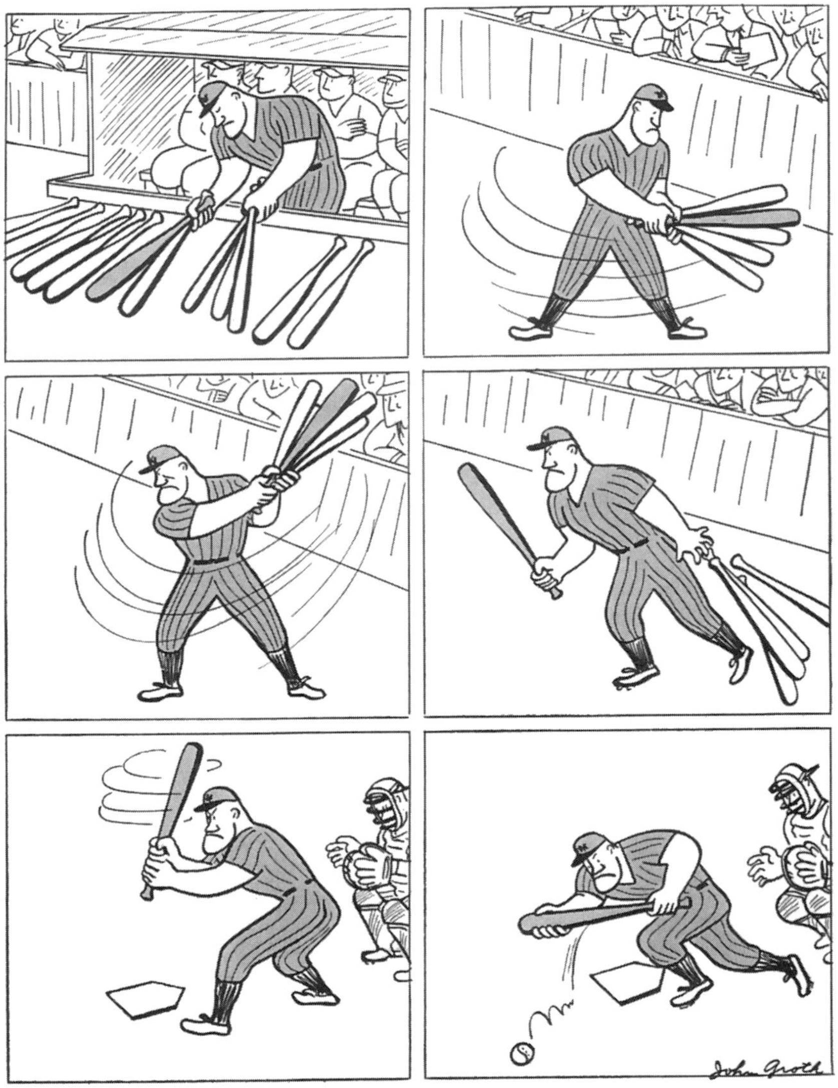
John Groth

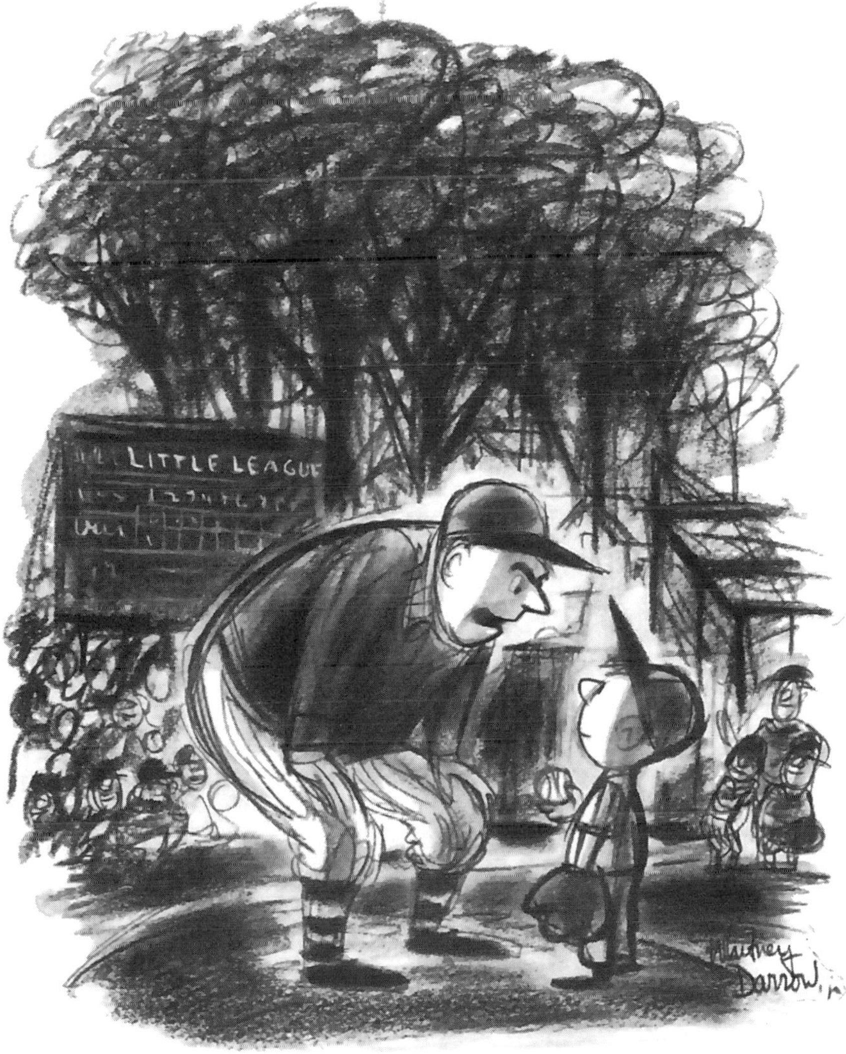
LITTLE LEAGUE

"Now, Randy, if a beanball was really bad, do you think the big major-league pitchers would use it?"

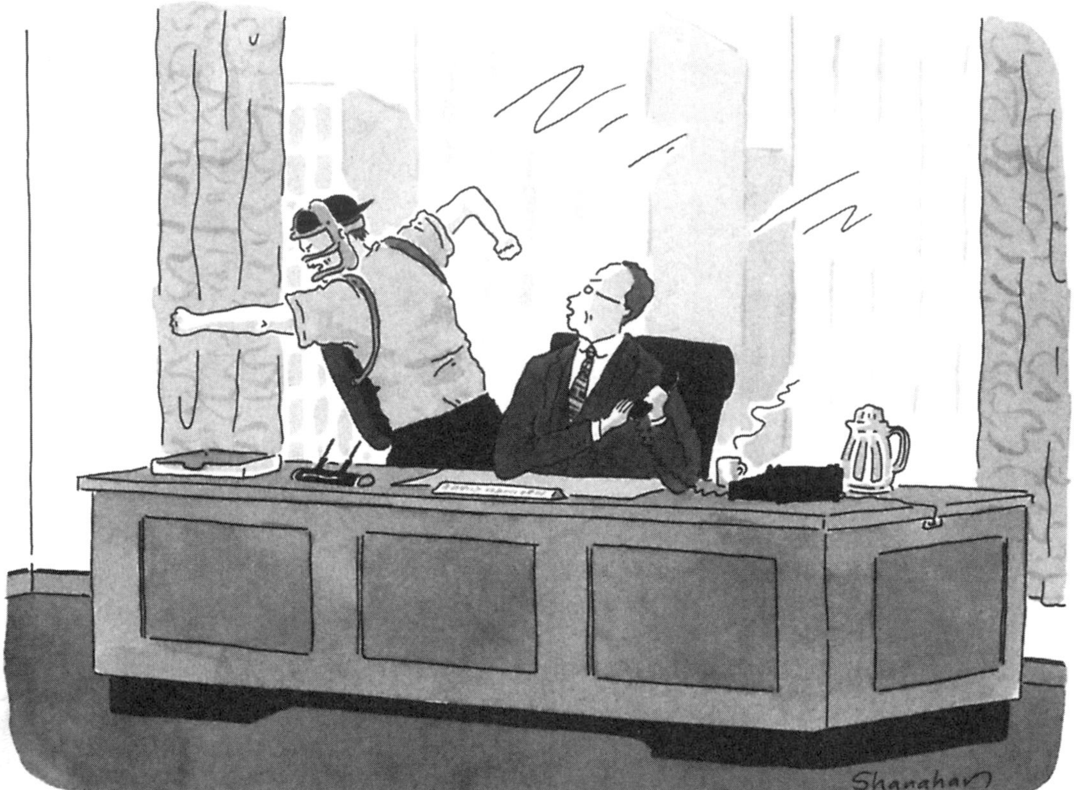
Shanahan

"Out? What are you, blind?"

NEW INDUCTEES

CHARLES LEROY BUMPUS
"BUMP"

DETROIT, A.L., 1961-1975
LEADS ALL CATCHERS IN TRIPS TO THE
MOUND, 5091. LED A.L. IN FEWEST MEN-
TAL ERRORS 6 YEARS. LED MAJORS
TWICE IN NUMBER OF WAYS HE CAN HURT
YOU (INCLUDES PINCHING, BITING, CLAWING,
KICKING, AND VARIOUS ABUSES TO MOTOR
VEHICLES). 4-TIME GOLD TONGUE AWARD
FOR FLAWLESS POST-GAME DICTION.

DARRYL HUTCHINS STILLPASS
"THE GUY"

CHICAGO, N.L., 1955-1969
HOLDS MANY N.L. RECORDS, AMONG
THEM: OUT-OF-PLAY BALLS TOSSED TO
SCREAMING FANS, 3012; DOUBLE-PUMPS
ON THROWS FROM RIGHT FIELD, 1619;
UNNECESSARY SLIDES, 3006. PIONEERED
USE OF AIR BAG TO REDUCE RISK
OF INJURY IN OUTFIELD COLLISIONS.

LAWRENCE MUTZ FOYLE
"MOP"

CINCINNATI, N.L., 1963-1978
LED N.L. IN BOO-INCURRING PICKOFF
ATTEMPTS 4 YEARS; FIRST MODERN
LEFT-HAND "SHORT MAN" TO LOWER
PANTLEG BELOW CALF. N.L. CAREER LEADER
IN SIGNS SHAKEN OFF, 6527. HOLDS
WORLD SERIES RECORD FOR MOST
APPEARANCES WITHOUT USING
RESIN BAG, 17.

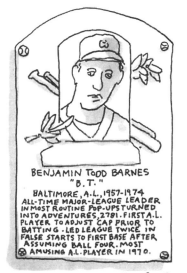

BENJAMIN TODD BARNES
"B.T."

BALTIMORE, A.L., 1957-1974
ALL-TIME MAJOR-LEAGUE LEADER
IN MOST ROUTINE POP-UPS TURNED
INTO ADVENTURES, 2781. FIRST A.L.
PLAYER TO ADJUST CAP PRIOR TO
BATTING. LED LEAGUE TWICE IN
FALSE STARTS TO FIRST BASE AFTER
ASSUMING BALL FOUR. MOST
AMUSING A.L. PLAYER IN 1970.

crawford

"If the Yankees move to New Jersey, will you be going, too?"

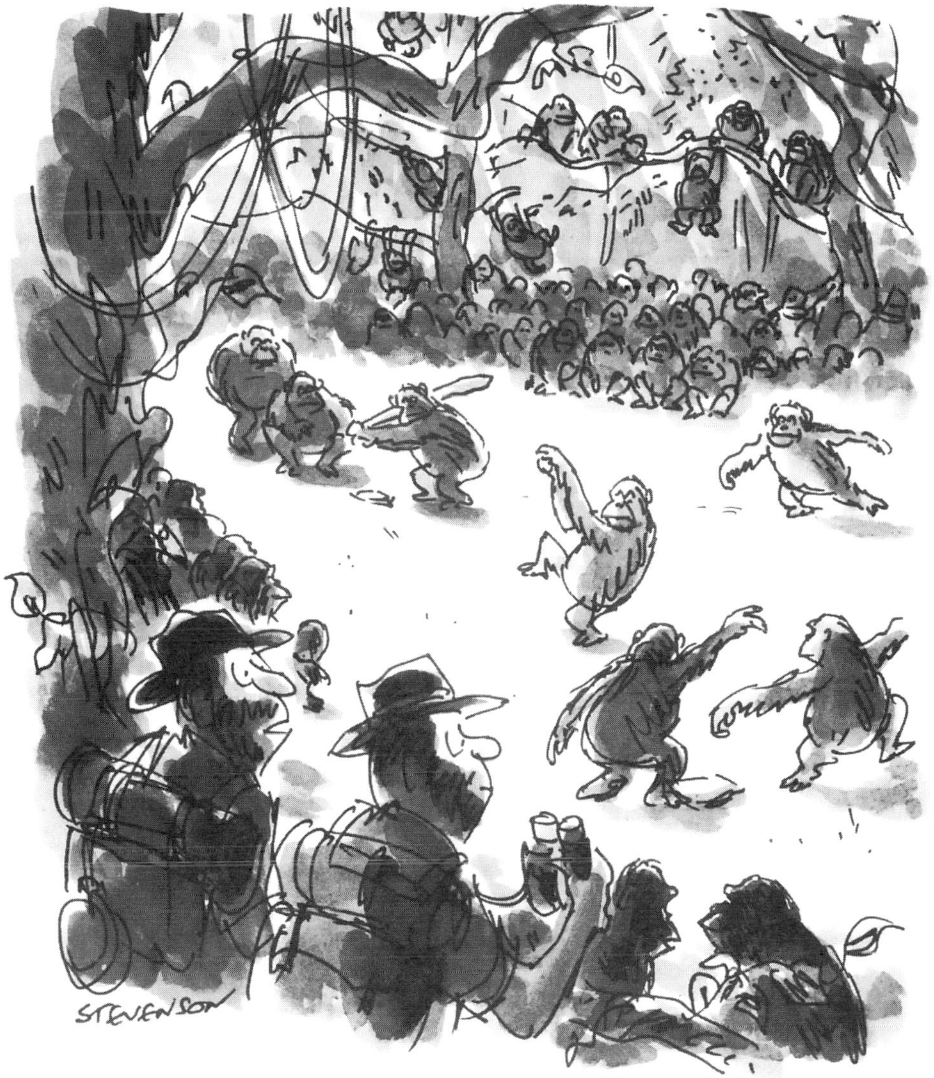
STEVENSON

"What's even more astonishing is it coincides exactly with the World Series."

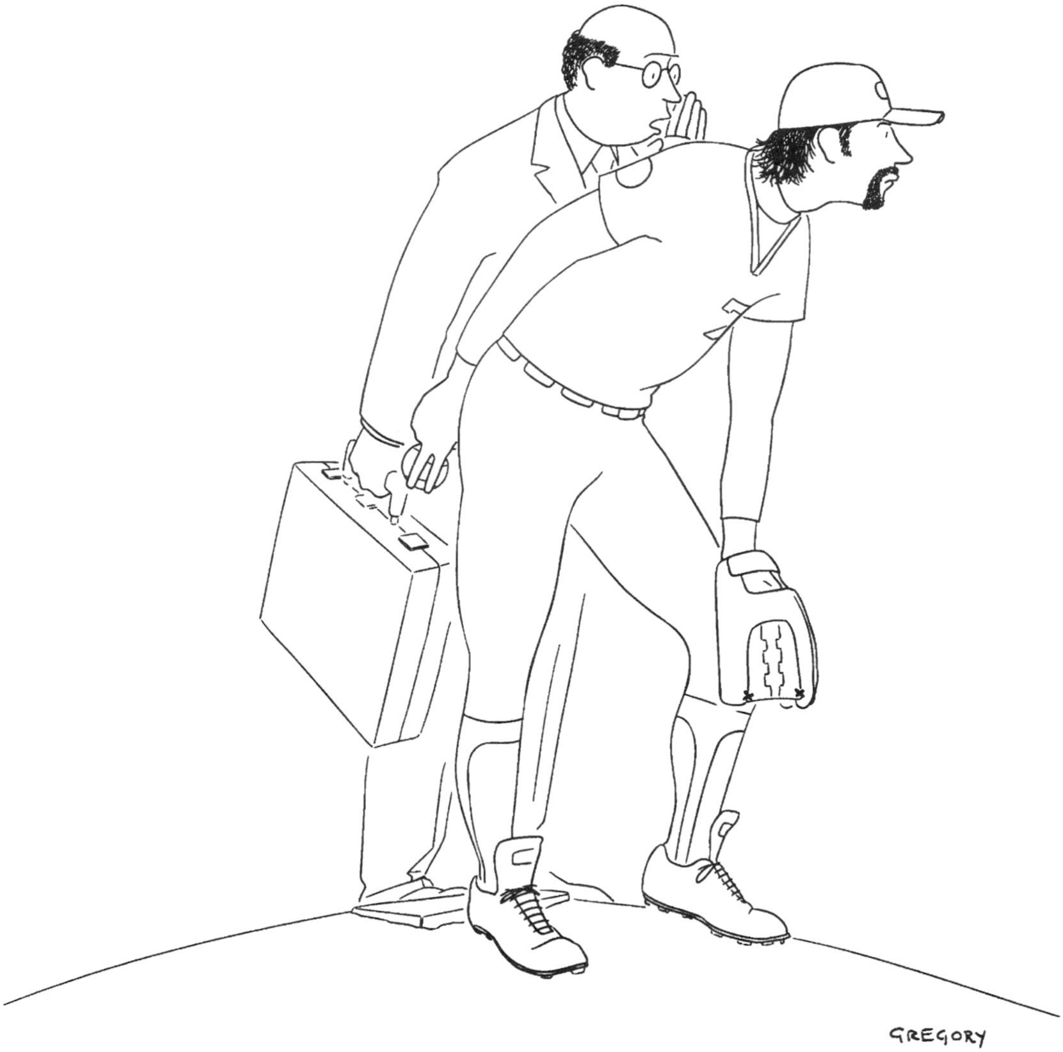
GREGORY

"As your attorney, I must strongly advise you against bringing the high heat."

"I *am* a little nervous. It's the first time I've ever pitched to two millionaires back to back."

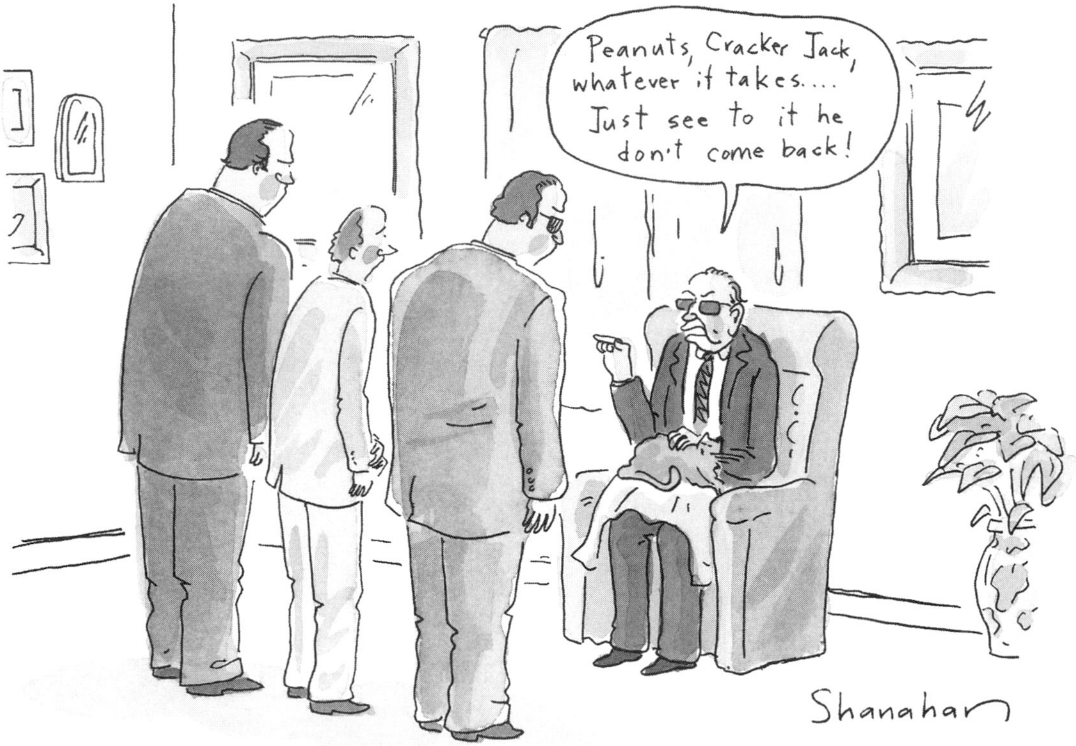
Peanuts, Cracker Jack, whatever it takes.... Just see to it he don't come back!
Shanahan

TAKEN OUT AT THE BALLGAME

"Gimme a hand—I'm stuck."

"*Mr. Foster is here. He just wants to touch base.*"

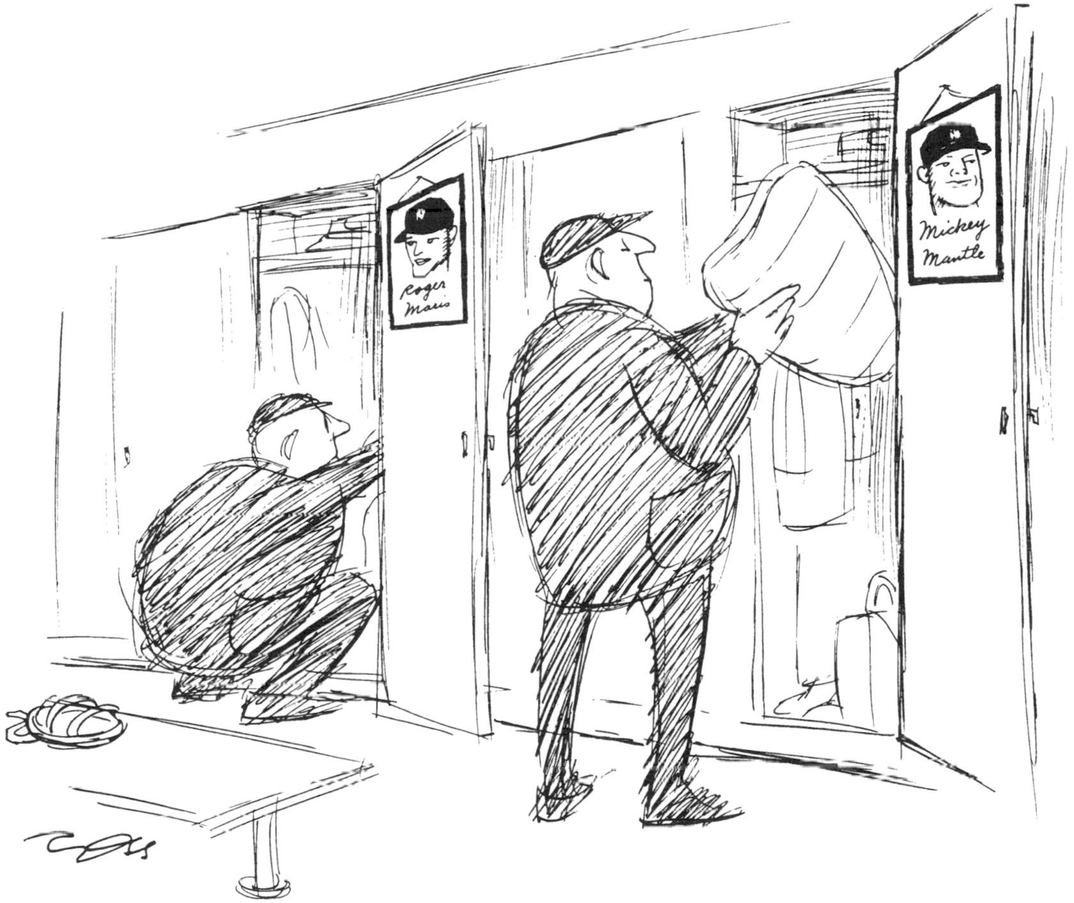
Roger Maris
Mickey Mantle

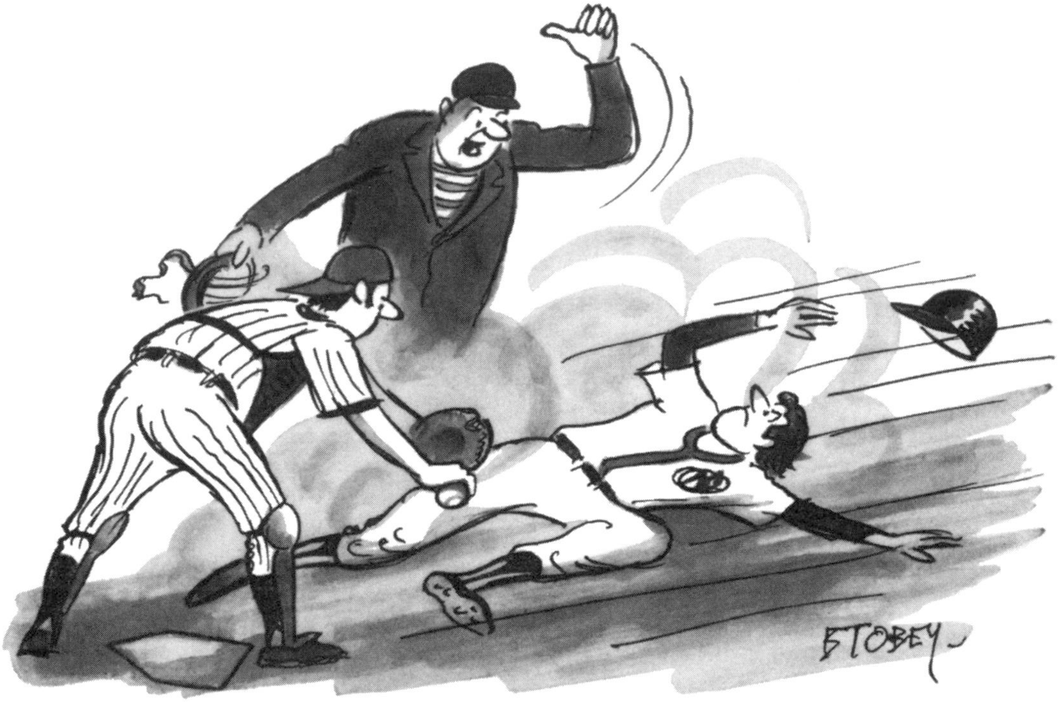

B TOBEY

"I don't know when I've seen a more magnificent slide. You're out!"

"No, Dad, I don't want to toss the old pill around."

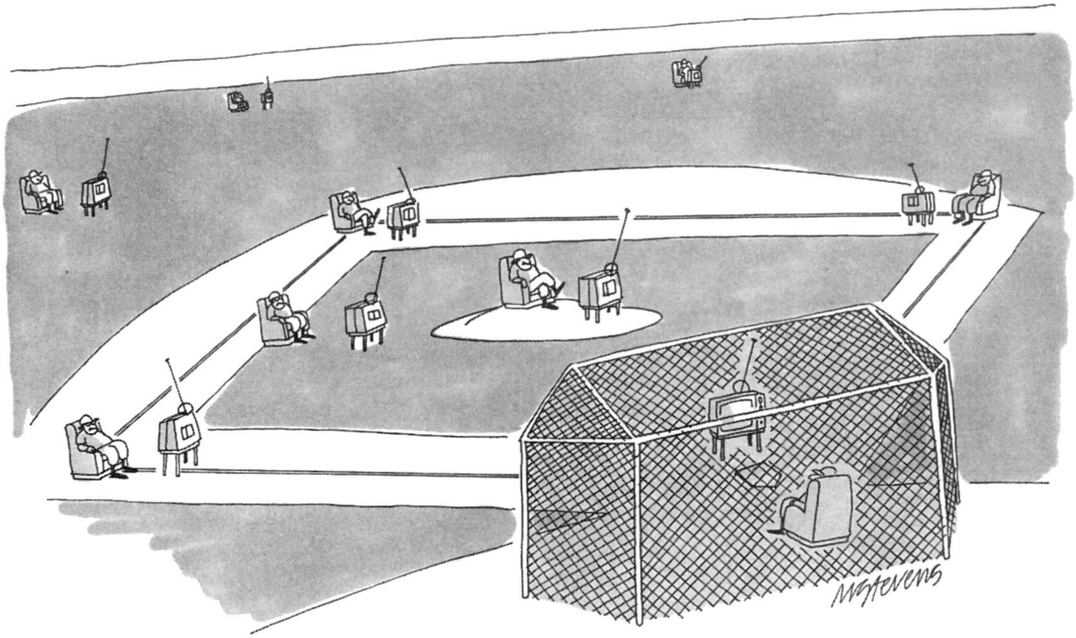
MStevens

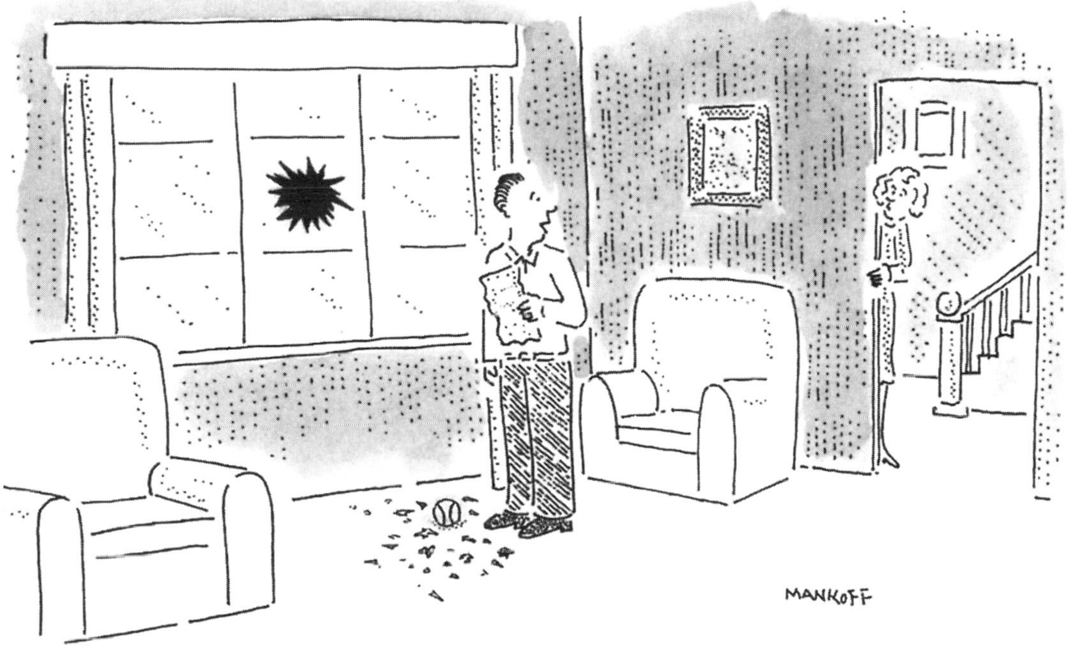
MANKOFF

"Why, it's a message from Major League Baseball."

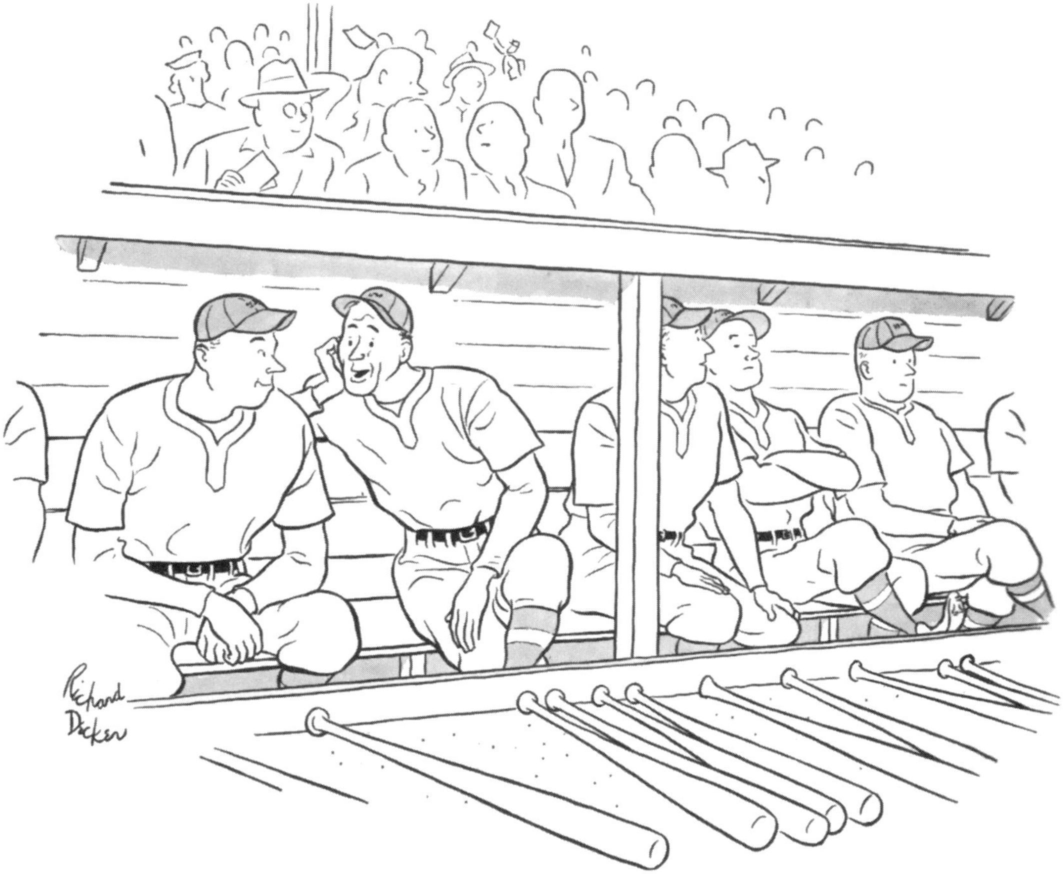
Richard Decker

"You know one thing I've always wanted—a summer vacation."

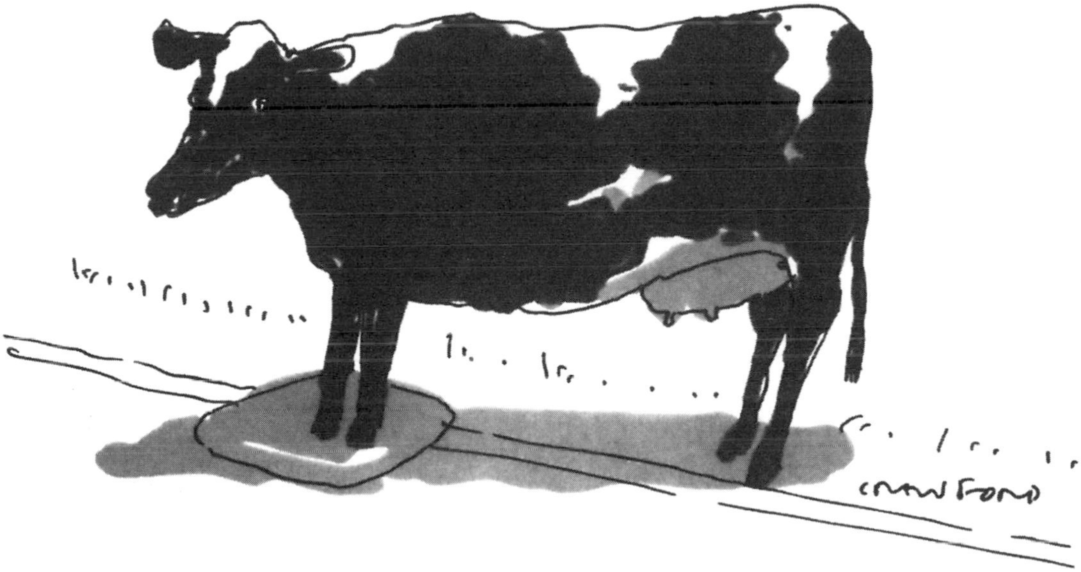
CRAWFORD

NO RUNS NO HITS ONE COW LEFT ON

EXECUTIVE SOFTBALL LEAGUE
SOMEBODY PICK THAT UP!
CBarsotti

"You are absolutely right—<u>World</u> Series is a misnomer. Now please shut up."

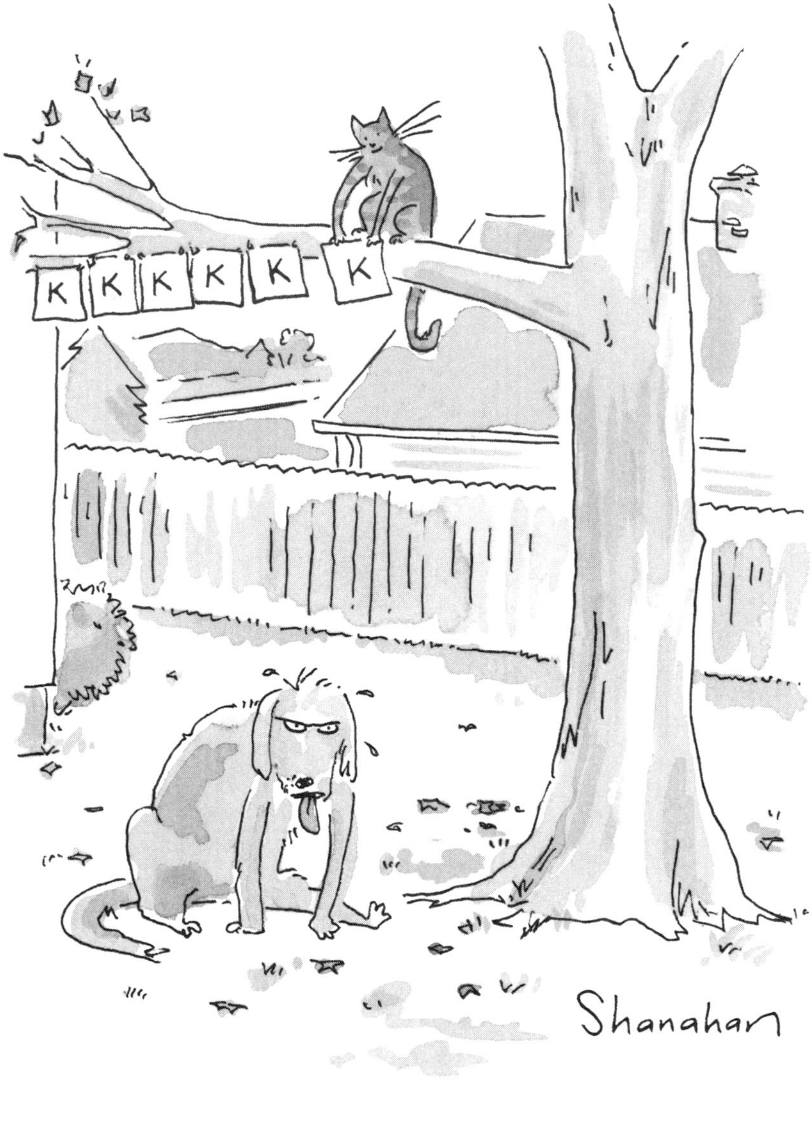
K
K
K
K
K
K
Shanahan

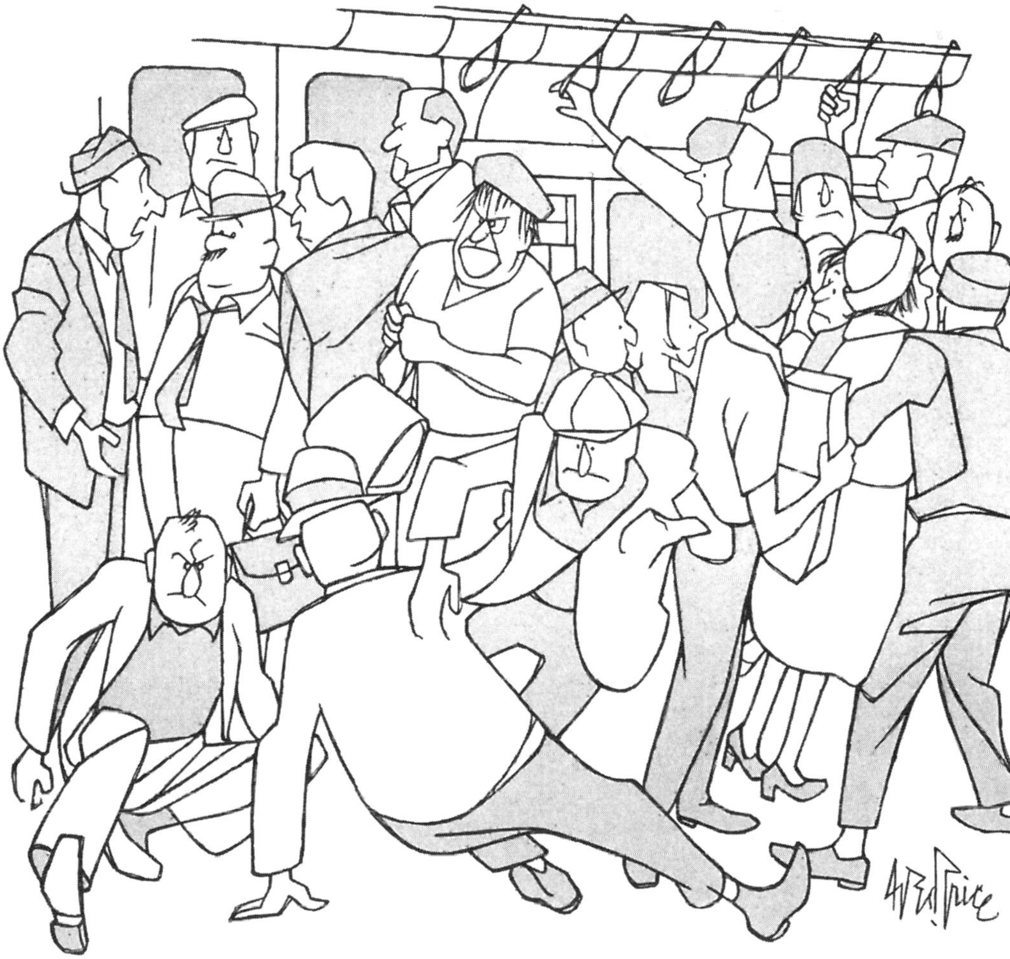
Alfred Price

"Why anyone should look forward to a subway series is beyond me."

"Got enough stuff for any six pitchers, but his control has me worried."

"*You can't talk to him like that, Herman! He makes your salary every time he trots lethargically to right field.*"

"I'm for the owners."

"Are there any here today who feel this union is not
in the best interests of baseball?"

"The boys don't seem to think much of Dolin as a hitter."

*"You will not argue. You are out. You will walk
quietly back to your dugout."*

"Don't sweat it. That's Little League—your dad comes, you choke."

"*Kellanay seems to be making real progress with his split-fingered fastball.*"

SPRING TRAINING

"*They all look promising enough, but I wish we had greater diversity.*"

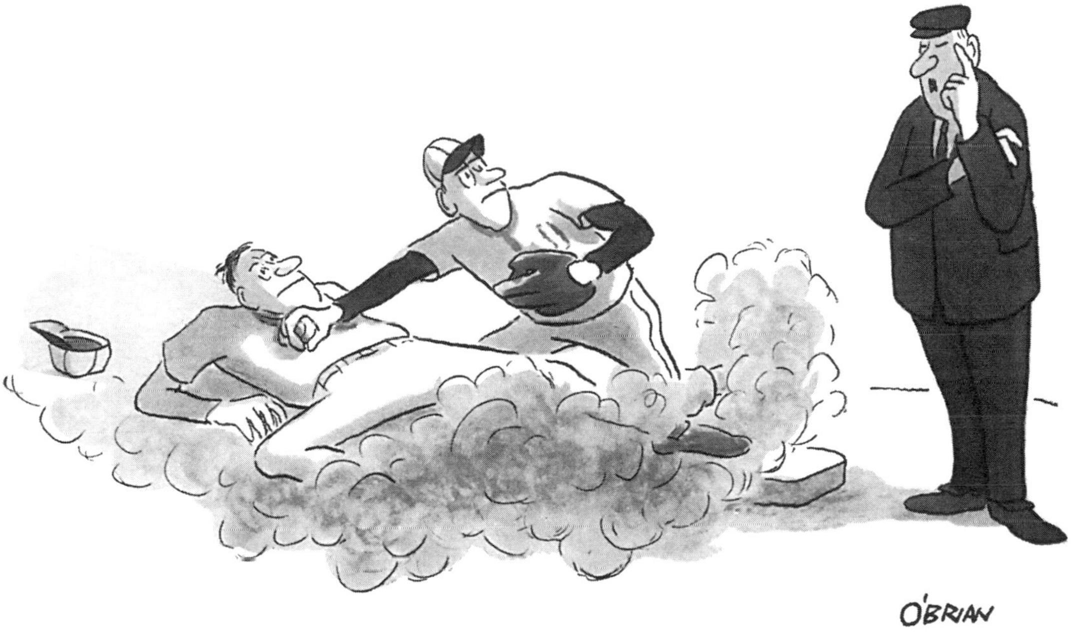
O'BRIAN

"I'm *thinking!*"

"I don't care if he *is* a baseball immortal. He should wear a robe and carry a harp like the rest of us."

"I came out O.K. Everything I had was in baseball cards."

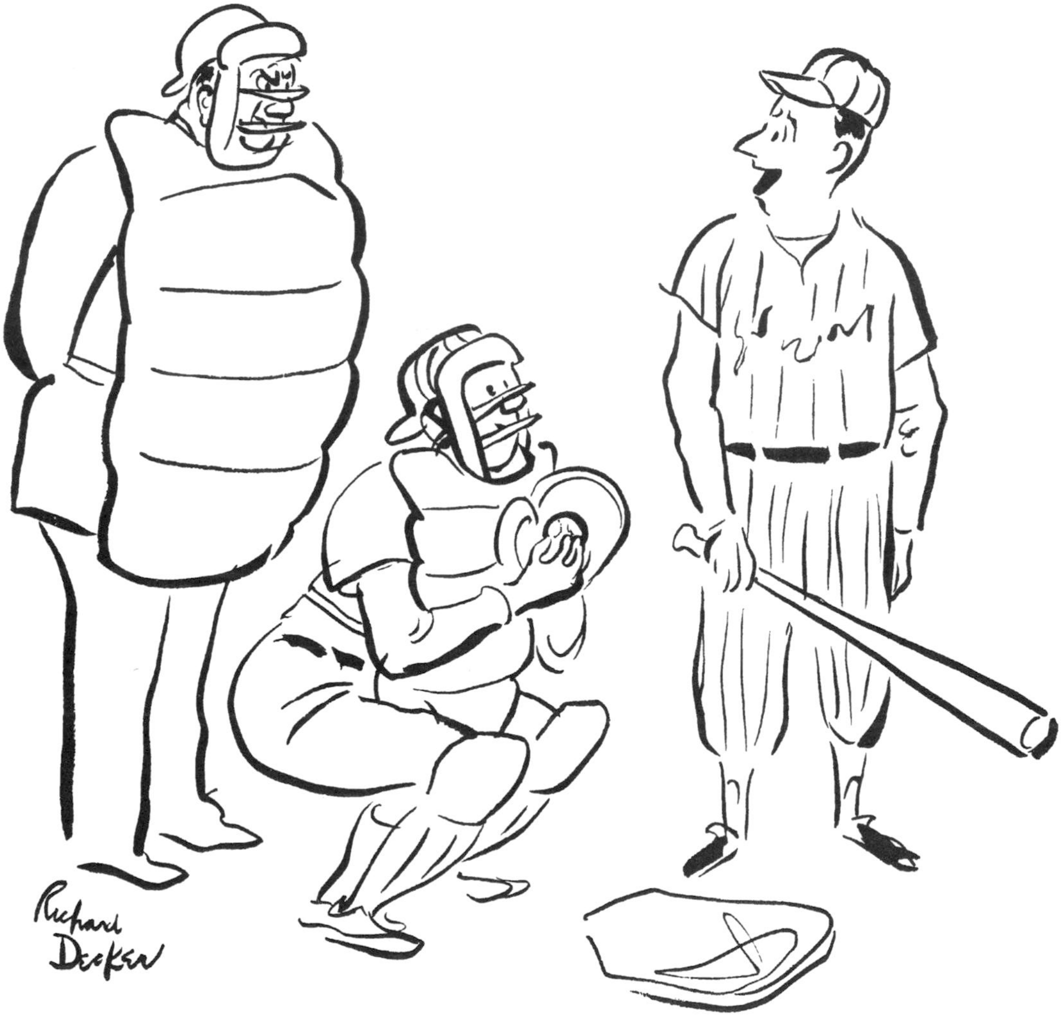
Richard
Decker

"Surely you jest?"

*"I suppose, as with most differences of opinion,
the truth lies somewhere in between."*

"*I was sent down to the minors and from there to Europe,*
and one thing just led to another."

SUN
RACQUETBALL
GOLF
BASEBALL
FOOTBALL
BASKETBALL
SOCCER
HANDBALL
TENNIS
SQUASH
D. Fradon

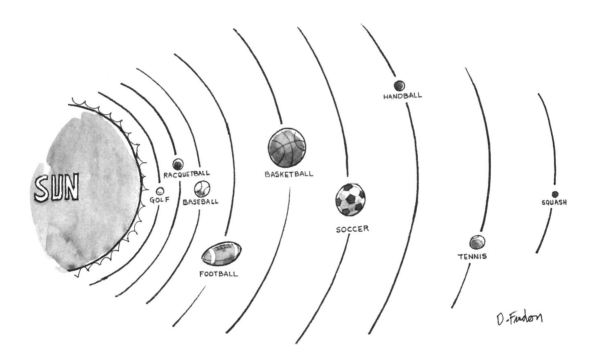

INDEX OF ARTISTS

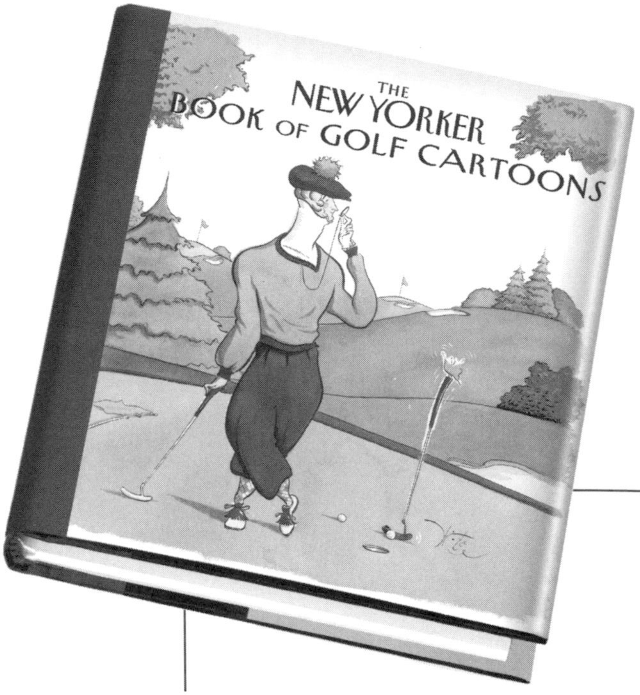

THE NEW YORKER BOOK OF GOLF CARTOONS

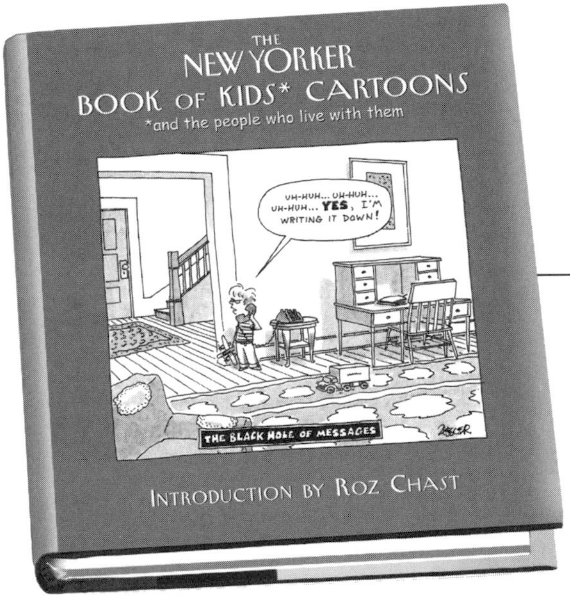

THE NEW YORKER
BOOK OF KIDS* CARTOONS
*and the people who live with them
UH-HUH... UH-HUH... UH-HUH... YES, I'M WRITING IT DOWN!
THE BLACK HOLE OF MESSAGES
INTRODUCTION BY ROZ CHAST

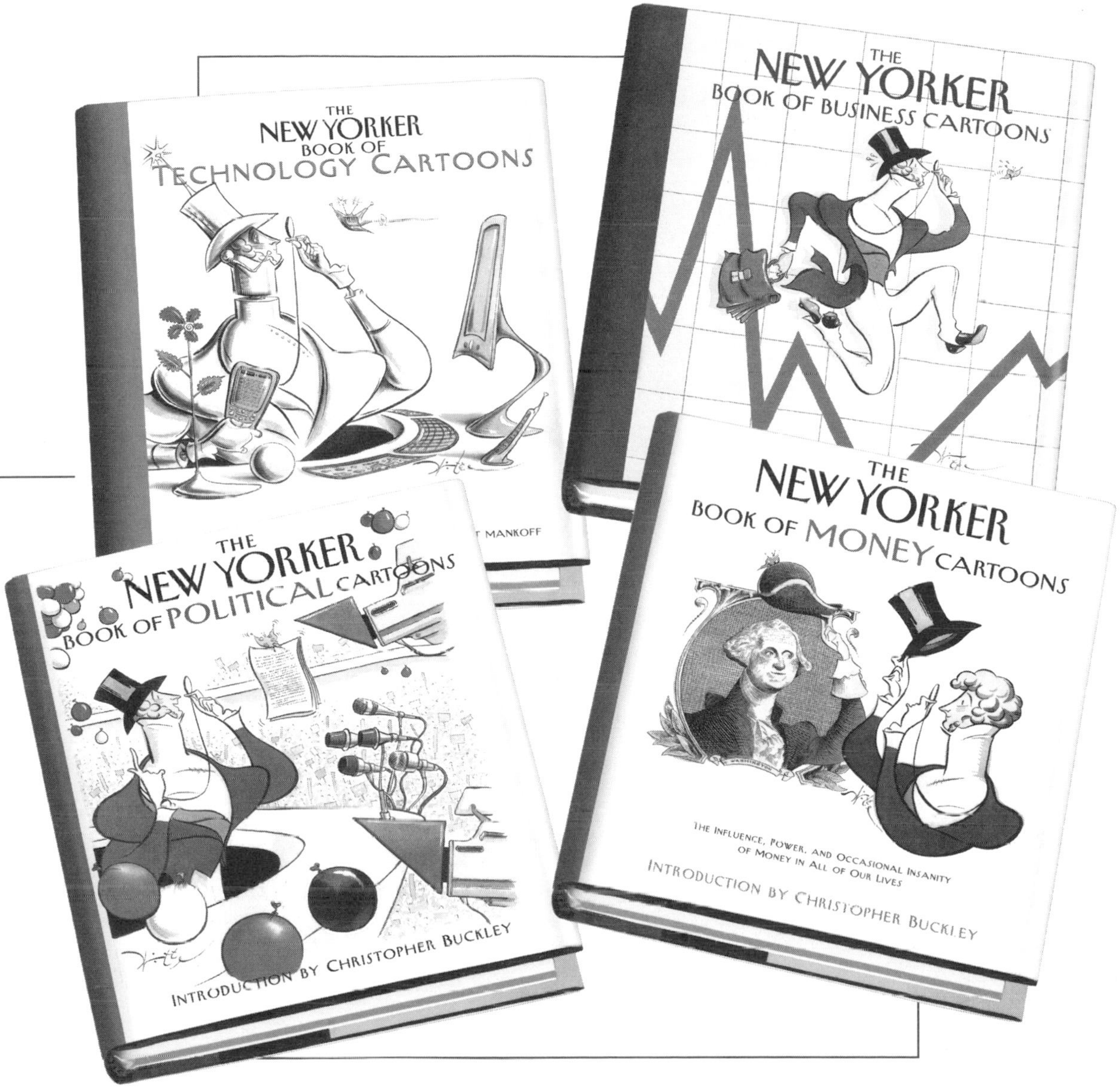
THE NEW YORKER BOOK OF TECHNOLOGY CARTOONS
THE NEW YORKER BOOK OF BUSINESS CARTOONS
THE NEW YORKER BOOK OF POLITICAL CARTOONS
INTRODUCTION BY CHRISTOPHER BUCKLEY
THE NEW YORKER BOOK OF MONEY CARTOONS
THE INFLUENCE, POWER, AND OCCASIONAL INSANITY OF MONEY IN ALL OF OUR LIVES
INTRODUCTION BY CHRISTOPHER BUCKLEY